Praise for
Little Mercies

Little Mercies is a spiritually uplifting book that teaches through a number of engaging stories of everyday people, everyday occurrences that God's grace is ever ready, ever present.

—*New York Times* and *USA Today* best-selling
author Debbie Macomber

Little Mercies is a delightful collection of simple, yet profound truths graciously offered to both challenge and encourage the heart. With tender honesty Lynn writes as one leaning across her kitchen table, grasping the hands of her guest and speaking words of hope, peace, joy, and mercy. Lynn will call you to find that pause in the busyness of your daily life. And if you answer her call, you will be rewarded with the authentic hope of a newer, richer rhythm of "little mercies" in your days.

—Fil Anderson, author of *Running on Empty:
Contemplative Spirituality for Overachievers* and *Breaking the
Rules: Trading Performance for Intimacy with God*

Reading Lynn Coulter's graceful, lyrical essays is like finding a new friend. She takes you to unusual places, introduces you to interesting people, and helps you see and hear things with new eyes and ears. Lynn calls herself "a pushover for heroic tales and long-ago stories," which explains her own storytelling gifts, leading you from real-life stories to biblical analogies in a subtle, seamless way. The woman can flat write.

—Liz Curtis Higgs, best-selling author
of *Bad Girls of the Bible*

Lynn Coulter's voice is a fresh perspective on two important ancient truths of the Bible—grace and mercy are the sustaining substances of a Christian life. When you read this book, you will be gently reminded of that.

—Ronda Rich, best-selling author of
What Southern Women Know About Faith

little mercies

CELEBRATING GOD'S EVERYDAY GRACE and GOODNESS

LYNN COULTER

PUBLISHING GROUP
Nashville, Tennessee

978-0-8054-4935-8

Published by B&H Publishing Group

Nashville, Tennessee

Dewey Decimal Classification: 231.8

Subject Heading: CHRISTIAN LIFE \ SPIRITUAL
LIFE \ GOD

1 2 3 4 5 6 7 8 • 15 14 13 12 11

This little book is offered in loving memory of
Emma Claire Key: proof, if ever it was needed,
that God's most precious blessings come in small packages.

Acknowledgments

As always, to Bill and Michael, with forever-love.

To Mary Wyman and Roseanne Key, whose friendships I cherish. Mary, thank you for walking alongside me as I wrote. I'm grateful for your encouragement, prayers, and insightful reading.

To Thomas Walters, who first welcomed me into the B&H Publishing family and introduced me to the good people who share God's Word with readers everywhere.

To my former editors at *Delta Sky*—David Bailey, Mickey McLean, and Britta Waller, and to publisher Duncan Christy: thank you for your excellent editorial guidance over the years. Some of the essays in this book appeared in *Sky* in different forms.

May God bless you, Kristi Cole and family, for sharing Brody's story. Brody taught us to celebrate every day of life, and his legacy is one of hope and faith.

Last, yet first above all, thank you, heavenly Father, for every good gift.

"I give thanks to my God for every remembrance of you, always praying with joy for all of you in my every prayer . . . because I have you in my heart, and you are all partners with me in grace . . ." (Phil. 1:3–4, 7).

Contents

*The LORD is good to all: and his tender
mercies are over all his works.*

—Psalm 145:9 KJV

Introduction

Thou has given me so much . . . give me one thing more, a grateful heart.

—George Herbert

How's your heart?

I'm not talking about your resting pulse rate or what kind of cholesterol meds you're supposed to take each morning. I'm talking about your spiritual heart, the place where your joy lives—or where it should live.

You've probably read what the psalmist once said about living a happy life: "This is the day the LORD has made; let us rejoice and be glad in it" (Ps. 118:24). But the truth is that real joy—that deep, unquenchable, wonder-*full* feeling that comes from knowing and loving God, and feeling him love you back—is missing from a lot of our ordinary lives.

And after all, what are we supposed to be so happy about nowadays? All we have to do is look around to see that we're living in a broken, fallen world.

Those of us who live in big cities know what it's like to crawl to work each day through heavy traffic, the skies as gray as granite overhead, and the air smelling of diesel fumes and other pollutants. Some of us are struggling to care for aging, ailing parents or to keep our young children safe in public schools and parks—worse, some of us are caught in a generation sandwich, trying to manage both at the same time.

Every time we spin the dial on the radio, we're reminded that threats to world peace and security abound in distant lands, and that frightening diseases are starting to hop from continent to continent almost overnight on commercial jets. In fact, there's so much bad news that it's fair to ask: Is there any other kind?

Yes, there is. There is some very Good News indeed, and it has a name: Jesus.

If you haven't met him before, it's time you were introduced. If you already know him, but you're living a life that feels weighed down with trouble or despair, then you need to know him a whole lot better. This little book yearns to help you do just that.

But let's agree on one thing right up front. No ostriches should read these pages. Even though I'm about to ask you to dive deep into the ocean of God's astounding love and immerse yourself in his endless, life-giving grace and mercy, we believers don't get a pass to bury our heads in the sand or hide our eyes behind our Bibles and ignore suffering and pain. As Christians, we are called to love and minister to a hurting world. It's our privilege to serve as good stewards of everything God has given us, so there's no ducking out or playing dumb here. We still have to pay attention to need wherever it exists and to work hard to clean up our messes wherever we find them. We have a calling to uphold; we are to live as faithful disciples. We're to love our neighbors as much as we love ourselves.

But while we do these things, I'm here to say that it's also time to stop talking so much about the bad stuff and to start living with a lot more joy.

In Italy there's a wonderful, progressive preschool that bears a motto carved over its entrance: "Nothing without joy." It simply means that whatever you're doing in life—*whatever* it is—you can do it with joy.

I know, I know. Some of you are shaking your heads right now, thinking that living with optimism is downright impossible. But remember, we're Easter people, and this is Sunday morning. The Friday when Jesus suffered and died is gone, behind us, its despair and darkness a thing of the past. This is a new day. We serve a risen, resurrected Lord, and because of Jesus, we have a choice, even when bad things happen or we live in tough circumstances, to meet each day with enthusiasm and energy; strength and courage; and wild, crazy, even inexplicable happiness.

Sadly some people are missing the good stuff because they don't see that the world is still packed with plenty to celebrate. Please know that I'm not pointing any fingers here. Just like a rubbernecker at a traffic accident, I can be as tempted as anyone else to focus on what's bad or alarming and to overlook what's right and good. It's easy to fall into a habit of complaining about how big our storm is, when we should be telling the storm how big our God is. I know, because I've done it.

Life can pummel us from all directions or stress us beyond belief, but be sure of this: Around every despairing corner, hope remains. Hope is at hand because Jesus is alive and he has conquered even death.

This book longs to encourage you to take a closer, press-your-nose-right-up-against-the-glass-and-be-amazed look at the world we live in, so you can discover more goodness and godliness in it.

Sure, it can be a challenge to see God's little mercies amid all the noise and anxieties. We can have bad days that pick us up like a sumo wrestler and slam us to the ground, and it's hard to recover our footing. We can find ourselves walking through a long and bitter season when pain and grief surround us and make us forget there was ever a better day. God didn't promise us easy lives. But he did promise to stick with us, no matter what, and he has sprinkled millions of tender mercies everywhere to remind us that he loves us and will never let us go.

So how do you find these little mercies, if you're not

accustomed to looking for them? Slow down, for starters. You'll uncover hidden beauty and unexpected blessings when you simply dial down some of the distractions and noise that surround you. Practice getting quiet. Make time to be alone, so you can read your Bible, pray, and discover what God wants you to know about life—*your* life. Pay attention to the small stuff, which turns out to be the significant stuff after all.

God really is in the details, as the old saying goes. He's the Artist who decorates a butterfly's wings with crayon-bright colors and dots a red-haired kid's nose with freckles. He multiplies the microscopic krill in the oceans so the whales can feed; lights up the dark with the silvery moon; and scatters the seeds on the wind to find a home in the earth and produce our flowers, fruits, and vegetables.

He puts the graceful curl in a snail's shell; the cool, soft feel in the grass under your bare feet; the brilliant red in a ripe tomato; and the honey in a honeycomb.

If you're not used to looking closely and living deeply, you may have to make an effort at first to find God's myriad small mercies, but don't worry. With practice all of us can grow grateful hearts.

Here's how I think of it. Have you ever had a scoop of bland, boring vanilla ice cream, and then noticed the guy at the table next to you eating a cone decorated with those rainbow-colored sprinkles? You're eating the same kind of ice cream, but you can tell from the expression on his face that he's enjoying his so much more because of those pink, green, yellow, and blue sugary treats.

Our lives may seem ordinary and plain, too, but they are sweeter than we can imagine when we realize that God is pouring his little mercies over the most vanilla-flavored days. It's the small things that make our lives richer and better. "Taste and see that the LORD is good" (Ps. 34:8).

Sure, the bad stuff gets the headlines and leads the six o'clock news. Daily we're rocked by reports of earthquakes and famine, divorce and disease. But Jesus came to give us a more abundant life *anyway*. While we plod through the muck and mud, nothing can displace, overtake, or overcome God's love and power. Nothing. No matter where we stand, in hardship or in plenty, we have hope because our heavenly Father is with us. The Scriptures promise: "The LORD is the One who will go before you. He will be with you; He will not leave you or forsake you. Do not be afraid or discouraged" (Deut. 31:8). How do we know this is true? We look around and discover his myriad mercies.

There's a great song from an old musical released in 1961, *Flower Drum Song*, that sums it up beautifully.[1] You can still find a copy of the movie, and even though some of its sensibilities feel dated and a bit cheesy now, the basic story, which is about the sweet romance between an Oriental boy and girl, is timeless.

Throughout the film the girl's old-school father does his best to keep the pair apart, determined to marry off his daughter to a rich man who has been chosen for her. She's miserable with this arrangement, although her devotion to her parent makes her obedient to his demands. But you can guess how the story ends; it was based on a Broadway play from the fifties, after all. The rich man finds a more sophisticated, worldly woman better suited to him, the rigid papa relents, and the boy and girl wind up with each other in a triumph of true love.

Aside from that happy ending, one of the most memorable things about the movie is its title song. Written by popular composers Rodgers and Hammerstein, the lyrics claim, "a hundred million miracles are happening every day."

It's true—God is sprinkling a hundred million mercies into our lives with each new morning. Look around. His grace is made manifest by the wildflowers in a ditch; the milky-white sweep of stars in the nighttime; and your little brother, all grown up, who still looks up to you in spite of the countless times you picked on him behind your mother's back.

Little mercies are the earthworms that loosen the rock-hard soil in your garden, the laughter we hear coming from a playground, and a second chance at anything. His grace shows up in our tears of relief; a chance meeting with a friend we haven't seen in years; and clean, fresh water pouring from the kitchen tap.

Tender blessings come in all shapes and sizes and colors too. Some show up as pets or animal companions; others are experienced just once, as strangers who touch our lives and then move on. God's gifts can be as small as a postcard from a friend or as big and extravagant as a sunset over the ocean. They can smell like tart lemons or fresh rain or the sweet, powdered nape of a baby's neck.

Tiny mercies are purring cats, good jokes, and love letters; restful naps, safe journeys, and clear weather for a high school football game on a Friday night. They are teachers who love to teach, a fish on your line, an open road, and songs and dreams and birthdays.

Life is hard, but God is good, and hope and joy come from learning to see, really see. That's what the late artist Georgia O'Keefe meant when she mourned once that nobody really sees a flower, because flowers are so small, and flowers take time to see and appreciate.

Despite everything that's wrong and worrisome, I've come to believe that the world is absolutely fabulous, packed down and overflowing with wonder and grace, some of it hidden just below the surface, like flakes of gold caught under the current in a mountain stream. The so-called ordinary stuff of life is quite extraordinary after all, when you recognize God's hand in it.

My prayer is that we can learn to pause in our busy lives and be grateful, that we can remember to celebrate the sweetness and honey that flow from God's hand. Life can be a challenge or a chore, but it's also bursting with bounty, beauty, joy, and adventure.

Take time to see, really see. Then count them, those hundred million miracles. To quote the song, they're happening every day.

The Hawk Lady

*I know every bird
of the mountains.*

—Psalm 50:11

No matter how closely you listen, you won't hear any soft chirps or coos or peeps coming from the birdhouses behind Monteen McCord's home about an hour's drive north of Atlanta. Then again, her birdhouses aren't the pastel-colored boxes with gingerbread trim that hang in most backyards, the fancy kind that invite chickadees and bluebirds to set up house-keeping with nests built from dried moss and straw.

Instead, Monteen's yard is the setting for a cluster of eight-foot-tall wooden outbuildings known as chambers, or aviaries. Think of the big outdoor cages that house exotic birds at many zoos and you're on the right track. The only difference is that Monteen's chambers aren't designed for public viewing. They're deliberately screened from nearby roads by a dense stand of pine trees and hardwoods, and that's much better for the occupants, who get nervous and unhappy when nosey humans venture too close.

While Monteen's birdhouses aren't like most birdhouses, Monteen herself isn't like most bird-watchers either. She's not content to simply look for birds with a pair of high-powered binoculars or coax them close to her windows with a dainty birdbath in the garden. Not for her, scattering handfuls of sunflower seeds to feed a hungry flock of gentle cardinals. Her backyard chambers are home to some of the fiercest birds in the natural world.

I met Monteen some fifteen years ago, when she was giving a demonstration about raptors at a local feed-and-seed store. It was hard to miss her—a woman clad in a Renaissance-style gown, sitting on a stool in the middle of a busy store, talking and gesturing with a huge, blinking owl perched on the leather glove covering her arm.

But then, Monteen is almost always accompanied by some kind of feathered friend, because she lives alongside dozens of raptors—predatory birds like barred owls, red-tailed hawks, peregrine falcons, buzzards, and ospreys—although her resident population can vary in species and number throughout the year. She has also housed crows, a baby turkey, and even a few vultures along the way (although serious birders debate whether that gangly-looking highway cleanup crew really belongs in the raptor category).

No matter. Monteen—she's simply Teen to her friends—is a passionate state and federally licensed wildlife rehabilitator who frequently helps or adopts birds that have been wounded, injured, or orphaned.

When she started her career a couple of decades ago, Monteen didn't envision a life spent mopping up after messy barn owls, stretching damaged wings in physical therapy routines, and administering medicines to stressed or cranky creatures with piercing beaks and razor-sharp talons.

Trained as a scrub nurse, Monteen initially worked for a plastic surgeon until, as she says, she grew tired of "doing nips and tucks for middle-aged, miserable, wealthy women." She chuckles, now in her own middle age, and sounds a bit wistful when she adds, "Now I wish I'd been more charitable in my assessment of them."

Disillusioned with vanity surgical procedures, Monteen eventually decided to quit her job and took a new position as a surgical assistant to a local veterinarian. The vet, as it happened, was a wildlife rehabber. One day while Monteen was working at his animal hospital, a hiker came in to ask for help. The man had been strolling through the woods when he came across an owlet that had tumbled out of its nest during a storm the previous night. One look at the magnificent little bird, now homeless and helpless, and Monteen says she was smitten.

Coming "nose to beak" with him "was an epiphany," she says. "Something about these birds is so incredible to me. He needed help, and I was going to move heaven and earth to make sure he got the best life he could."

With the veterinarian's encouragement, Monteen began studying predatory birds, making newfound use of her knowledge and skills in anatomy and physiology. Raised by a father who hunted game for the family table and later inspired by a romantic movie about the medieval era called Ladyhawke,[2] Monteen eventually took her passion for raptors a step further and became a certified falconer.

With a lot of concentrated study and hands-on practice, Monteen passed the rigorous comprehensive exams on raptor biology and health care that are required to take part in this legendary "sport of kings" and started working to obtain her own rehabber permits. (Since raptors are migratory birds, they are rigorously protected by both state and federal legislation.) It took seven years of apprenticeship under an expert sponsor to earn the prestigious title of master falconer. It's a rare title for a woman to hold, and today Monteen is one of a few thousand women in the United States to possess it.

Then Sam, the bird I met that day in the feed store, came into Monteen's life. Sam is a great horned owl, a handsome, winsome, tawny bird that has been with her for more than sixteen years now. He lives in a backyard chamber, too, but his home is a specialized "condo" rigged with two perches and an extra stretch of flying room. Although he's in excellent health, Sam can never return to the wild. Because he was found as a baby and kept too long by well-meaning humans, Monteen explains sadly, he never learned to hunt or fend for himself. He simply isn't capable of surviving on his own.

Armed with multiple hard-won permits and licenses, Monteen decided to take Sam on the road with her to educate children and adults about wild birds, and they now work together in a nonprofit educational program Monteen founded called HawkTalk. The pair visit schools, Scout meetings, civic groups, elder hostels, and many other kinds of organizations where she gives live bird-of-prey demonstrations and lectures.

Sam loves to travel with Monteen, riding shotgun in the passenger seat, while other birds that appear in the HawkTalk presentations usually ride in spacious cages in the back of Teen's old, donated SUV. Glimpsing a great horned owl through the windshield makes for a lot of double takes from passing drivers, which both Monteen and Sam enjoy.

One summer afternoon I followed Monteen into her woods to meet her newest adoptee. When we stopped at a big chamber shadowed by the setting sun, she motioned for me to peer inside. "Just don't press your face up against the screen," she warned, as I tried to see into the darkened interior. I stayed back but squinted hard and finally made out a small figure clinging to a tree branch nailed to one wall.

"Whoo-o-o cooks for you?" the occupant crooned, spotting us. He tilted his head to give us a curious look. Two soulful eyes, dark brown as chocolate bars, peered back at me.

"This is Snake Davis," Monteen said by way of introduction. "I named him for this crazy Atlanta DJ I like to listen to on the radio. He's my new barred owl." I leaned closer to admire his softly striped brown and white feathers and watched his talons tighten their grip on the branch.

Suddenly Snake gave a snap of his raincoat-yellow beak, and I understood why Monteen had cautioned me to stay back from the thin wire that separated us. This owl, his hooked beak as sharp as the point on a can opener, was capable of puncturing a tin can or biting off an intruding nose.

"He's gorgeous," I murmured—because he was, in all his fierce beauty.

Monteen thought so too, but then, she's madly in love with all her birds. At any one time she might host a dozen who need help before they can be released into the wild—if they can recover to be released at all.

Snake blinked his eyes and clacked his beak again, a sign that meant he was feeling defensive. While wild birds are not pets, and never should be, like most of her raptors, Snake would eventually allow Monteen to handle him. She has an uncanny gift for handling furred or feathered creatures, and she's able to forge a bond with most of them through time, trust, and patient training.

As you might guess, her rehab work and the educational program require a tremendous amount of money, physical work, and commitment. Running a small charity is demanding, especially when funding dwindles during lean economic periods. And however beautiful the hawks and owls are, however much Monteen enjoys sharing her life with them, there is nothing simple about their care. It takes a strong stomach just to feed them.

"These birds don't eat cereal and Greek salads," she says pointedly. She regularly makes a fifteen-hour run to collect mice donated by an out-of-state research lab and stores them in one of four big freezers in her home until the mice are needed for meals.

If this kind of work isn't for the weak of stomach, it isn't for the faint of heart either. Skill and courage are needed to handle birds that are at the top of their food chain. "But they're important," she says. "Imagine how overrun we'd be with rats and rabbits if God hadn't made raptors to keep them in check."

And she dotes on them. Monteen loves each and every bird for its unique personality and antics. Besides Snake, she's fond of Scully, a green-eyed screech owl with a deformed beak, and a gawky buzzard she adopted after the little girl who watched over his egg until it hatched was astonished to discover that he wasn't a chicken. Their photos are displayed as proudly as family portraits on her living room walls, and like any devoted parent, she regales visitors with stories about their adventures.

Sam, who has been her companion and coteacher longer than any other bird, is frequently invited into the house to sit on Monteen's lap while she watches TV, or to hang out on the back of the sofa. Like any couple who've been together for a long time, the two occasionally wrangle over the remote control. At every opportunity, Sam likes to stuff it under the couch cushions.

I'm always caught between laughter and wide-eyed admiration for Monteen. She's smart, funny, fearless, plainspoken, and self-reliant. I never know if I'll find her with her hair dyed dark red for a late-night rocker gig (she likes to sing with a band of friends) or dressed in medieval garb and falconer's gear with a live falcon in tow. Her love for wild birds is her mission, and although she'd probably hoot with laughter if I said this to her face, I believe her life demonstrates a rare and special grace.

It takes grace to muck out a dirty, smelly aviary, or dodge the speeding cars on a busy highway while you drag to safety a bird that has just collided with a passing car. It takes charity to sweat and strain to chip the mortar and bricks out of a crumbling chimney in an abandoned farmhouse to free a few trapped barn owlets whose mother wasn't choosey or smart about her nesting site.

Grace is nursing a dying falcon, dribbling drops of water down her throat and sitting with her until the last breath is sighed, so the patient won't pass alone, or trying to persuade overeager developers to spare a tree that's filled with a nest and nestlings. It's teaching kids that not all of the marvelous creatures God has put into the world come with bunny-soft fur and friendly dispositions, but they are no less marvelous simply because they have feathers, sharp beaks, and fierce eyes.

Some people may look at Monteen and think she's small change. She's only one person, after all, with a sputtering old vehicle, some beat-up birds, four basement freezers packed with donated lab mice, and a meager budget. To say she gets by on a wing and a prayer is no joke. What is one hawk, after all, in the grand scheme of things? What does it matter if she tries to save a tiny screech owl or one homely, wattle-necked buzzard? What is the value of one bird in such a vast and varied universe?

"I know every bird of the mountains," we are told in Psalm 50:11. The Bible is filled with stories about birds, and there's nothing small or insignificant about any of them.

In the first chapter of Genesis, God commanded the seas to team with fish and the skies to be filled with birds, and the Creator looked on them all with pleasure.

When John, that rough prophet who shouted in the wilderness, baptized Jesus in the Jordan River, the Holy Spirit soared out of heaven and took the form of a humble dove that rested over Jesus' head. God chose that little dove over any other creature to serve as a symbol of peace and gentleness, to publicly show the great joy he took in his only begotten Son.

Another prophet, Elijah, once hid himself near Cherith Brook, in a spot east of the Jordan River, as God commanded, and survived because God used the ravens to send food for him. Fed on the bread and meat the birds carried in their beaks and claws, Elijah was able to endure his trials until God told him to move on. God sent those black-winged ravens to let us know he is able to provide for us in any circumstance, and that he can, and often does, use even the most unassuming, seemingly insignificant member of creation to do it. Because of those ravens, we recognize God as the sovereign Ruler of the natural world.

The Scriptures don't stop there. They speak of vultures and mighty eagles, of turtledoves that sing sweet love songs, and fat quails that miraculously appeared in a harsh desert to save a people from starvation as they made their exodus out of Egypt.

When floodwaters raged over the face of the earth, it was a bird that Noah sent out to search for dry land, and he watched with hope until it returned with a sprig of greenery, a sign that crops could grow and people could establish their homes again. Jesus, in describing his great love for Jerusalem, compared himself to a mother hen who longed to gather her chicks under the tender shelter of her wings.

And, of course, there are the sparrows. "Even a sparrow finds a home, and a swallow, a nest for herself where she places her young—near Your altars, LORD of Hosts, my King and my God. How happy are those who reside in Your house, who praise You continually," said the psalmist (Ps. 84:3–4).

In Matthew 10:29 we're reminded that God is aware when a single sparrow falls to the ground, so why, then, should we fear? If he watches over the smallest birds, his attention and love is fixed even more firmly on us.

The book of Luke assures us that our heavenly Father will provide for our needs, just as the glossy black ravens are fed, even though the big birds don't sow a garden or reap a harvest or store any crops in barns.

None of the tender mercies that God shows are burdensome to him; none of it is duty for our Abba. He never grows weary or tired of caretaking, and he never forgets our needs, because he loves us. Our Father "delights to give [us] the kingdom" (Luke 12:32).

God is our helper and healer when we, like Monteen's owls, hawks, or falcons, are broken, hurt, or alone. He ministers to us through his Son, Jesus, when we are at our worst, and when we are weak, his strength holds us up. He feeds us on his Word.

What amazes me, in light of God's deep devotion for us, is that he's also willing to allow us to accept him or walk away. It's similar to what we parents have to do, when it's time to give our children wings. We still love and pray for them, of course, but when they're old enough, and we've done our best to raise them, we know we have to let go. We may watch as they drive away to college or jobs in distant cities with our hearts thumping and our breath held, but we do stand aside. We realize that they have to make their own choices if they're going to live true and authentic lives. We want them to find their heart's desires, the things that give them independence, joy, and purpose. God wants us to live with passion and freedom, too, and that's why he lets us choose who—or what—we will serve.

When Monteen has done her best; when a falcon's fragile bones have knit, or an owl's missing feathers have grown back, or a damaged beak has healed; when a bird has learned to hunt and fend for itself—however much she has come to love it; and she does love each and every one—she takes the bird into the woods and releases it into the wild. Letting go is hard. After the long days of nurturing, feeding, and healing, the bond has become strong.

"Rhonda, my very first wild hawk that I used in falconry, shared a physical bond with me that was almost palpable," Monteen says. "But when I released her three years later, she immediately reverted back to the wild. I would see her working the pond or pasture and go out with the lure and whistle and try to call her down. She would have none of it."

Imagine God, watching over us and tenderly caring for us every day, yet always giving us the freedom to leave or to abide.

Watching one of Monteen's wild birds take flight is like seeing a bit of grace, a reflection of God's infinite, precious love, launched into the sky on two strong wings.

2

Night Music

Shout to the LORD, all the earth; be jubilant,
shout for joy, and sing. . . . Let the sea
and all that fills it, the world and those
who live in it, resound.

—Psalm 98:4, 7

*T*here's nothing wrong with my ears, but my hearing isn't all it should be. My family often complains that I zone out when I'm focused on something important—say, updating some profile for my favorite online store or printing a bookstore coupon that just popped up in my e-mail. To test me, they throw out weird stuff in their conversation, just to see if I'm really listening, and to be honest, most of it usually flies right by me. It's only later, when I wrap up whatever I'm concentrating on, that their words finally sink in and I realize I've been nodding and mumbling, "Yes, sure," when asked if I want goldfish for dinner.

I don't mean to be rude. It's just that the world is filled with so many distractions and so much noise, I can't concentrate unless I tune out and drill down on whatever task is at hand. I'm not like my son, who has to have the TV on when he's doing homework, or his friends, who feel undressed if they venture out without a cell phone in hand or headphones over their ears. Blame it on my inability to multitask, if you will, but there it is.

On the other hand, my friend Mary excels at paying attention. We met many years ago, when both of us were expecting our first babies and trying to endure one of Georgia's sizzling-hot summers, when the combination of heat and humidity made it feel as if every breath was taken through a wet woolen blanket.

Mary's baby, a girl, arrived first, in August of that year, while I plodded on, whalelike and nauseous, until my son was delivered in early November. Before long we bonded with each other almost as closely as with our newborns. Neither of us had family living nearby, so we learned about parenting together, swapping books about how to cope with colic and trading tips on diaper rash. And we strolled.

With little Emily in her stroller and Michael in his, Mary and I pushed our babies 'round and 'round the neighborhood, walking off our baby fat (she was way more successful than I was), laughing, and sharing. We were a good team, practically a matched set. Until the unthinkable happened.

Mary's husband, Jim, came home one night with the news of

a big promotion, one that would take the family clear across the country, from their Atlanta home to Seattle.

"I'm so happy for you," I cried to Mary. Inside, I just cried. *Don't leave me*, I wanted to wail. *You're like a sister to me now, and I need you.* I thought about Emily, sporting her first teeth, two tiny, white Chiclets on her lower gum, and how she was starting to babble through her drool, and how I'd miss the next first thing she did, and the next and the next.

Mary probably didn't know how closely I was watching her for cues, but she was teaching me a lot. I hadn't been around babies in decades—I was one of those rare teenage girls who somehow managed to miss the babysitting routine—and I was flailing, trying to figure out what to do when Michael kept waking up every two hours, which of course meant I woke up every two hours too. I didn't know how to do so many baby things, and she was showing me, both with and without words, how to be a mother.

But the best we could manage, when moving day finally arrived, was to promise to write to each other in those pre-e-mail days, when long distance phone calls were too pricey for mommies whose babies kept quickly outgrowing their tiny shoes and Onesies.

In the first few letters Mary penned from Washington State, she admitted that the adjustment was hard. They had bought a beautiful new home with brilliant, overhead lighting in the spacious kitchen, but in the beginning Seattle's constant cloud cover and drizzle seemed oppressive. It felt dreary, she said, after living for so long in the sunny South. As the seasons changed, she wrote about going to shop for downy parkas and boots and mittens.

The New Year came and went. As the weather began to warm up again, Mary wrote me about missing the signs of spring back in Atlanta. There were no dogwoods blooming in the Pacific Northwest, she said, and she missed a special stand of April daffodils that used to pop up in our neighborhood, where we'd posed our babies for their first Easter photos. She was also forgetting how the old neighborhood sounded when she used to sit outside on warm, pleasant nights.

"Send me a tape recording," she wrote one day, and I pictured her sitting at the table in her bright kitchen, Emily playing at her feet. "I need something to listen to. Seattle doesn't feel like home."

A recording of what? I wondered. We had managed a quick few phone calls on our limited budgets, after all, so I didn't think she meant my voice.

As it turned out, she wanted to hear a little night music. "When the weather warms up," she explained, I was to open my back door and listen. She missed the croaks and peeps and chirps and whirs that came from the woods behind our homes. "Southern nights," she said, "have a sound all their own."

And so, armed with a tape recorder, I picked out a foggy, froggy kind of night, an evening when a quick spring rain and cool air had conspired to fling a veil of mist over the lawn.

I dragged an aluminum lawn chair into my backyard and settled in, stretching my legs out in front of me, as I punched the start button on the machine and waited.

I sat there in the darkness for a while, the black sky overhead punctuated only by a dim necklace of street lamps and the blink of lights from some passing planes. I didn't hear anything at first. I closed my eyes when I finally realized that I didn't need to see to find what I was looking for.

I had to only listen and try to filter out the hiss of the tape sliding through the old recorder. A few cars drove by, tires whooshing over the damp street, but finally I heard it.

The night was singing or, at least, the creatures in the grass and woods around me were tuning up. This wasn't birdsong, but something different. I caught the whistled, bell-like calls of spring peepers, tiny frogs common to marshy areas in the South.

Thanks to the field guides I like to read, I recognized other voices in the choir. I heard the stutter of chorus frogs, like the sound of fingernails clicking over the teeth of a comb. Still other frogs and toads honked and rasped, barked and trilled and croaked. Unseen bugs—I felt plenty of them biting my bare legs—buzzed and whirred around me.

I taped for a long time, and after that night I made other trips into the backyard to sit and listen to the evening's entertainment. By midsummer new players had joined the symphony. Field crickets came out to chirp, rubbing their rough wings together.

Katydids shouted their names: "Katy-did, Katy-didn't." Cicadas sounded a loud, electric buzz from the treetops, a zinging noise that flew up and down in volume, as if an unseen hand was playing with a radio dial. Grasshoppers hopped up and bounced off my ankles as I sat in my lawn chair, and even after I chased them away, I heard them sawing their legs back and forth, like violinists drawing their bows over taut strings.

I mailed the first tape recording to Mary, but I kept one or two more tapes for myself. Sometimes, replaying them during the day, I caught sounds I'd missed. I discovered that if I paid attention, I could hear the swish of pine branches in a strong wind or the snap of a twig in the woods behind my house or the patter of heavy raindrops on the leaves of our magnolia tree. Often I heard the low pulse and rumble of summer thunder in the distance.

"It's great," Mary said when she called to tell me her tape had arrived. "I'm sitting out here on the back steps in the dark, listening to it." I pictured her there, wrapped in a sweater in Seattle's evening air, holding the phone to her ear. "It's getting cold again," she added, and I heard a clatter from the wind chimes that swung on her deck.

Like Mary's family, my family eventually moved away from the old neighborhood, too, and although many years had passed since Mary was my neighbor, I felt sad to leave the place where I'd met my friend. It seemed almost as if we'd keep our close connection as long as we still lived there. I knew I'd also miss the chorus singing in the dark woods.

Since I taped that first recording for Mary, I've come to believe that every inch of creation is singing, in one way or another.

The reclusive little poet Emily Dickinson once compared hope to a bird, a "thing with feathers," that lives in the soul and "sings the tune without the words and never stops at all." But hope isn't the only thing that sings. Everything that has breath is squeaking, rasping, whirring, and croaking, and it's all part of that "tune without the words" that testifies to a divine Creator.

The symphony has been going on since the beginning. Adam and Eve were the first ones to hear "the sound of the LORD God walking in the garden at the time of the evening breeze" (Gen. 3:8). God spoke through the natural world even then, and it's easy to imagine the swish of his footsteps through the tall grasses in Eden, and the buzz and hum of bees in the trees and wildflowers.

Author Frederick Buechner has written that we're put into the world through God's grace, and no matter how small and insignificant we may feel at times, we're actually the guests at a celebration being held in our honor. Our lives are part of a party that God throws every day, and without us—well, as Buechner says, the party just wouldn't be complete. Everyone has a role and a reason for being here, and everyone has a note to sing in the concert, whether we're silver-throated divas or raspy amateurs.

All God desires is that we lift our voices to sing "glory," to give praise and thanks to the One who makes the darkness and the woods and, yes, even the biting bugs, which have their own fluttering, downright annoying roles to perform. Even if our human voices were stilled, Jesus once told his disciples, the very stones would cry out, telling of God's glory and power (Luke 19:40).

I thought I'd never see my friend Mary again, but more than a decade later God revealed that he had other plans. She called one day, out of the blue, to tell me that her husband had landed another promotion, and this time, they were coming back to Atlanta. We made plans to meet after they found another house, and although we don't live next door anymore, we visit as often as we can. The only difference is that now we compare our children's college courses and romances instead of their earaches and nap times.

Throughout the years we lived so far apart, Mary sat in her backyard in Seattle and I sat in mine in Atlanta, listening to the crickets, frogs, and wind, and we prayed for each other. Although we never felt it in a physical way, I believe the Holy Spirit was blowing through our hearts during that time, sustaining and guiding us as we raised our children, loved our husbands, managed our homes, did our work, and missed one another's friendship. Maybe the Spirit's voice was part of the music I heard in the darkness.

As often as I can, I still make time to sit outdoors by myself and listen. God is speaking words of love for his creation through those soft murmurs and chirps. He's communicating his power in the croaks and trills that come out of the woods, lakes, and mountains. That rough music of the earth made his presence known in the beginning, even as it makes him known to us today.

Fly-Fishing

*Then He took the five loaves and the two fish, and
looking up to heaven, He blessed and broke them.
He kept giving them to the disciples to set before
the crowd. Everyone ate and was filled. Then
they picked up 12 baskets of leftover pieces.*

—Luke 9:16–17

I'll admit I'm not a sportswoman. I love the outdoors, but most of my nature experience has been limited to mild-mannered spectator stuff, like bird-watching from the front porch or raising tomatoes and cucumbers in my vegetable patch. I've done some camping (in an air-conditioned RV that boasted plug-ins for electricity and running water), and I've gone tubing down an icy north Georgia river (in a bubble-gum pink inner tube, which knocked a lot of the "wild adventure" bragging rights out of the trip).

So the truth is, when an editor from a travel magazine called one day and offered me the chance to go to Montana and cover an all-female, fly-fishing weekend, I didn't stop to think about the physical challenges of paddling down a swift river or trying to unhook a slippery fish from my line. My first thought was that hunky actor Brad Pitt had visited almost the same spot back in 1995, while making a film called *A River Runs Through It* and that the movie had been directed by equally hunky actor Robert Redford. Shot on location on the Yellowstone and Boulder rivers,[3] the film was based on a critically acclaimed novella by author Norman Maclean and followed the story of a Presbyterian minister who shared his love of fly-fishing with his two very different sons.

I practically had my bag packed before the ink dried on my contract, but eventually I settled down—after all, Brad and Bob weren't still out there, hanging around on the riverbanks, and in that kind of wilderness setting, I was more likely to encounter a bear than a Hollywood star—so I determined to focus on the editor's instructions. This article was supposed to describe a personal quest. In this case, my quest as a woman was to understand and experience a sport that has appealed primarily to men in the past.

Before I left my home in Atlanta, I prepared by interviewing a few fly-fishing fans. Why, I asked them, are you so passionate about this sport? From what I knew, it seemed to inspire an unusual degree of devotion among its practitioners.

True to the spirit of Maclean's book, most of the men and women I spoke to described fly-fishing as kind of a spiritual experience, a chance to reconnect with something or Someone greater than themselves while they practiced the ancient art of casting a line over a cold, clear river. They felt a kinship with the natural world, they confided, in voices that were both hushed and reverent, every time they spotted the flash of a rainbow trout or walked in the shadow of a rugged mountain, and being outdoors gave them a rare chance to rest and relax. They found peace on the river as they fished. That sounded like a sort of worship to me, although the walls of their "church" were only tall, green trees, and the ceiling of their sanctuary was just a sweep of high and fleecy clouds.

Spiritual fishing—what an odd concept. I hit the library and the Internet and discovered, to my surprise, that one of the earliest and most influential books about fly-fishing was penned in 1486 by a member of a religious community. Even more surprisingly, the writer was a woman.

Although some historians still debate her very existence, Dame Juliana Berners, a noblewoman who became the prioress of a nunnery in St. Albans, is generally credited as the author of the *Treatyse of Fysshynge wyth an Angle*.[4] The good woman's book was among the first to set out a code of ethics for anglers, and it encouraged readers to pass along their love of fishing for others. Did Berners really pen this classic work? We can't be sure, but if she did, I was intrigued that even a cloistered, fifteenth-century woman would be enamored of this sport.

In late August, I booked a flight into Bozeman, Montana, and then connected to a puddle-jumper, a small plane that delivered me to the West Yellowstone airport. From there I drove another forty miles to an isolated lodge that sat yet another forty miles away from the Montana western entrance to Yellowstone National Park. When I stopped for gas—according to the signs, the last gas station before the long drive to the lodge—the owner, who sold me peanuts and a soft drink, recommended making any last-minute phone calls before I got back behind the wheel. Where I was headed, he said, there weren't any cell towers.

I arrived at the lodge late in the afternoon, worn out from the time zone change and my long journey, and wolfed down some dinner as I tried to make the acquaintance of a half dozen other ladies who had also signed on for the novice fly-fishing weekend. We met our guides, too, all young guys with friendly spirits, and all dressed in plaid shirts and khaki pants, who told us to set our clocks for dawn.

It didn't take long to get our feet wet, so to speak. The next morning, while we gulped down cups of coffee to fortify ourselves in the cool morning air, the guides loaded our gear into their trucks. The men divvied us up quickly, eager to get on the river, and I found myself riding shotgun in a red pickup. A nice selection of hand-tied flies was stabbed into its headliner and a fistful of bird feathers stuck out from behind each visor. John, my driver and guide for the day, spotted me immediately for the humble worm fisherman that I was and grinned as he assured me that he'd unhook any flopping fish I managed to catch.

Although the guys gave us a quick demonstration of basic skills before we launched our small, three-person boats, showing us how to flick our rods behind us and cast our lines forward with one smooth motion, I snagged my line in a bush on the bank on my first try and every practice cast thereafter. It was sad, especially since Brad Pitt had made it look deceptively easy with his graceful loop and swirls. I felt my heart swell with pity for the day John had before him.

Over the next eight hours I whispered several prayers of sincere thanks that John displayed one of the fruits of the spirit—in my case, extreme patience—as he cheerfully rowed our boat through choppy waves and stopped repeatedly to untangle the countless snarls I hacked into my leader line.

"Give the line time to get behind you, before you cast forward," he instructed—over and over, because it took me awhile to figure out that the point wasn't to land a fish as fast as I could. Nobody, he explained, was there to rush me, so I was supposed to take time to set up my cast, especially since I was thrown off balance by the snappy wind at my back, the rock of the water, and the new skills I was striving to learn.

Eventually I got the idea. Fly-fishing wasn't about speed, as John said, and it didn't take muscles. It was about timing and paying attention to the behavior of the fish. "It's about solving the puzzle," John said, explaining that a fisherman needed to know which bugs were hatching on the river, so he—or she—could use the right lure. The fish weren't dumb. They sensed the season of the year and would rise to bite only an insect that would normally be active at that time. That's why, he said, a successful fisherman needed to know when to use a down-wing silhouette or a hand-tied nymph, or how to spot a bubble down-stream that meant a trout had just taken a fly from the surface of the water. So far John was picking the right lures for my line, but I seemed to be doing everything else wrong. Fly-fishing was a lot more demanding than the bank fishing I'd done back home with a cardboard tub of red wigglers. "When you catch a fish, it's an affirmation of your work," John said, as he encouraged me to keep trying.

And so I worked and worked to catch a fish, and surprisingly I began to enjoy myself once I found a rhythm and felt the power of a good cast, which flowed down my arm and out into the slen-der rod. As the boat eased downriver, my casts grew smoother, and I relaxed into the peace of the day, just casting and drifting as John rowed.

As I fished and we floated, I looked around at the boats filled with the other women and their guides. My initial theory seemed wrong. I'd thought that the women who signed up for this weekend had come only to follow in a boyfriend or hus-band's footsteps, and I'd doubted their genuine interest in wad-ing into an icy pool to fish or learning to tie tinsel and elk hair into a homemade fly.

Well, I was partly wrong anyway. Some of the women on this all-ladies' trip admitted that they wanted to learn this sport so they could spend more time with their menfolk, who were going fishing with or without them. But the rest of us were fast discovering what the men already knew: Fishing takes you into beautiful places, and it can be both art and pleasure.

I landed two little fish that afternoon, and in keeping with the strict regulations that protect the waters and the wildlife of the Madison River, John carefully unhooked and released them. I had to also release my dream of dining that night on pan-fried trout basted in lemon and melted butter, too, but I was willing, since supporting conservation on the river was more important than my growling stomach.

I flopped into my bed at the lodge that evening, feeling like a beached fish myself, and rose before sunrise the next day for one more lesson. As soon as my boat pushed away from the bank, ably rowed this time by a guide who called himself Big Fish Brett, the elusive trout began to hit.

Tall, lanky, pony-tailed Brett exuded a vibe of cool detachment behind his mirrored sunglasses, which was enough to intimidate me as he seated me at the front of his boat, facing downriver, and took up his post at the oars behind me. I tried to relax as the waves thumped against our hull and the paddles squeaked softly in the oarlocks.

Brett rigged my line with a bug-like lure that resembled a black and white spider with striped legs, and soon began shouting instructions to my back. "Cast near the bank," he yelled against the wind, which was rising. "Good, good," he said when

I complied. Suddenly my strike indicator jumped, a sure sign that a fish had risen to take the lure, and laid-back Brett started hollering with excitement. "Hit it! Hit it!" he cried, which meant I was to jerk the rod and set the fish.

He was as pumped as I was when I finally landed a respectable sixteen-incher, and as soon as we'd snapped a quick picture with the camera I'd stowed under my seat, he gently unhooked the trout and lowered it back into the tea-colored riffles. He let the fish rest and waited until its gills filled with life-giving water, then opened his hands, patiently waiting until it decided it was ready to swim back into the stream. I watched, elated, as the trout took off with a flick of its tail.

As the day progressed and the sun beat down overhead, I landed a few more small fish, until the guides called a halt and we all jumped out to pull our boats onto a spit of graveled land. We helped lug gear onto the shore as Brett passed around sandwiches and cold drinks for our lunch, and leaned our backs against some shade trees to rest while he and John pointed out migrating Arctic terns on the river and a flock of mergansers paddling past.

Our guides were too tactful to say it, but as I watched Brett polish off a sandwich in two bites and stride out into the river in his scuffed and worn wading boots, I knew that teaching a bunch of beginners had to be pretty tedious stuff for these experienced fishermen. Clearly they'd taken this job to stay close to their sport, so they could dip a line in the water every now and then, and I wondered how they kept from becoming frustrated and annoyed when we novices kept fumbling over their simple directions.

Of course the best teachers always have to show patience with beginners. "Come, follow me," Jesus once said to a similar bunch of newbies, "and I'll make you fishers of men" (see Matt. 4:19). Over and over Jesus instructed, counseled, and encouraged the inexperienced disciples he'd plucked from a host of other professions, as he taught them the skills they needed to catch elusive human hearts. A word my grandmother used came to me, and it applied to this experience: long-suffering. Jesus was long-suffering in his dealings with his disciples. Patience, it seemed, was born from grace.

As we watched the men on the river, I thought about how, after a long night on the sea, Jesus' followers encountered him after his resurrection. They had seen him die; what kind of hope did they have left by then? Small wonder that after they'd fished all day, and still drew up nothing but empty nets, they were ready to haul their boats ashore and quit.

But Jesus called out to them before they got to the beach and urged them to try again. This time, he told them, cast your nets over the right side of the boat.

Peter and the other men, not recognizing their risen Lord, were discouraged and exhausted, but something in their hearts responded to the authority of his voice and words. They slung their nets out just once more.

Because they were willing to obey, the Scriptures tell us, the fish began to hit. At last their net was filled with so many flopping, flipping fish, it was too heavy to haul into the boat.

The disciples must have been awestruck with their catch. They must have stared at the man on shore with their eyes wide and mouths open, asking each other, *Who is this guy?* How did he know what to do, when they, the seasoned, experienced fishermen, had failed?

The disciples didn't waste much time asking questions. They simply realized, in that moment when they felt the netted weight of the struggling fish, that this man was a guide worth following, and more. He was *the* Guide, their own Lord, come back again.

I love this story, because it shows that a life with Jesus is about abundance, but that it's also a reminder that the right guide can take you wherever you need to be and teach you all you need to know.

Yes, it's also about a bunch of slippery fish. Jesus showed up at the end of a long, tiring day, when a few men, sweaty and stinking from the smell of bait and saltwater, were ready to go home. But Jesus wasn't fazed by the lack of fish the men needed to feed their families or to sell in the marketplace. He simply stepped up and gave them the direction to go back into the water and try again. He was the source of their provision, the leader, the teacher, the Savior, just as he is ours today.

When Peter and the other men finally recognized Jesus,

they joined him on the shore, where he built a charcoal fire and cooked a meal of fish and bread for them to share. They sat together on the sand, warming their hands in the cool night air, and although they likely ate until they were full, there was probably plenty left over.

We share Communion in our church, of course, but anytime that I'm able to sit down and take a meal with friends, I am reminded of Communion from which all true blessings originate. The food I eat, the fellowship I belong to, all emanate from one sacred Source.

It was this sense of appreciation for the abundant blessings that come from and through Christ that I felt, when I sat under the shade trees with John, Big Fish Brett, and the other women, all of us damp, sunburned, and sweaty, sharing sandwiches and cookies that tasted faintly of river water and grit. Upstream we watched as an otter quietly slipped into the Madison and swam away. My muscles ached, and I got up to wash my hands in the water where the brown trout and the cutthroats made their homes. Jesus once stood on a shore, not graveled like the one under my feet, but hot and sandy, waiting as Peter and his friends rowed for home. He was there to share a meal and himself with them. I felt his presence, too, standing by that beautiful river, reveling in a good day just ended. Our guides told us to collect our gear, and we turned to follow them, grateful and glad for all we had learned.

Singing behind the Plow

*Whatever you do, do it enthusiastically,
as something done for the Lord and not
for men, knowing that you will receive the
reward of an inheritance from the Lord—
you serve the Lord Christ.*

—Colossians 3:23–24

When a young New Englander named John C. Campbell and his bride, Olive Dame, hitched a mule to their wagon in the early 1900s and headed into the southern Appalachian Mountains, they were carrying some big dreams along with them. Mountain folk were among the poorest in the country in those hardscrabble days and, largely because of their poverty and physical isolation, among the least likely to have a formal education.

John and Olive were much different. Students of social reform, education, and theology, they had heard about harsh living conditions in the mountains and felt called to help. Even though they'd been married only a short time, the couple packed up their household goods and headed into the hills on a mission of service wherever they found a need.

"[Campbell] was an incurable do-gooder," says Jan Davidson, the director of a folk school that the Campbells eventually helped establish at the foothills of the mountains in Brasstown, North Carolina. "[He] felt he needed to learn the truth about mountain people, who they were, and what they did."

The couple must have felt as if they'd landed on the moon when they first arrived in the region, where the locals still spoke Chaucerian English, although "nobody could read a lick," as Jan says. Olive and John began their work by collecting data on the poor-but-proud descendants of Scots and Scots-Irish settlers. While John studied the mountaineers' farming practices, hoping to improve the quality of their lives by teaching them new and better agricultural methods, Olive visited with the families in their primitive log cabins, where she sat each night around a different stone hearth or kitchen table. By the eye-straining light of flickering oil lamps, she copied down their old Appalachian ballads and painstakingly wrote down the instructions the families gave her for making their traditional handicrafts, like quilts and wooden bowls.

John and Olive fell in love with the people they met as they moved from town to town, traveling all the way from Georgia into West Virginia, and soon the couple agreed that the region needed some sort of school. Perhaps, they said to each other, they could launch a "school for life" based on educational methods they'd studied and learned about abroad. In those so-called folk schools, students didn't compete against one another, and there were no tests and grades. They simply learned for the sheer love of learning. This unorthodox educational style encouraged students to achieve their personal best, without having to measure themselves against each other. These kinds of classes sounded bold and exciting, but sadly John died in 1919 while the school was still only a dream.

Grieving but undeterred, Olive didn't give up. She took time after John's death to travel with a friend, Marguerite Butler, to visit some of the schools in Europe, Denmark, Sweden, and other countries whose educational ideas she hoped to copy. By the time the women returned to the United States, they were determined to establish a unique learning center styled after a Danish *folkehojskole*, or "folk high school," for their impoverished mountain friends. But they faced a huge problem. The price tag for such an institution would be high.

Olive and Marguerite decided to present their idea to the residents of Brasstown first, where they met with a group of interested locals. The school, the women explained, was going to require land and cash to get started, as well as building materials and physical labor, and the townspeople themselves would have to provide these things. Classes would be taught, they said, using a Danish method known as the living word. It encouraged students to learn by talking and discussing, rather than by reading books and writing papers, and primarily people would learn by doing. Everything at this school would be hands-on.

Was it too much to ask people who often went barefoot because they couldn't afford shoes to help build a school whose goal, the ladies explained elegantly, was to "awaken" and "enliven"?

Would these hardworking poor care about becoming "enlightened" when their families and neighbors frequently died from malnutrition or the lack of decent health care?

The answer was an enthusiastic yes. Mountain people cared very much. When Olive and Marguerite returned to the community a few weeks later to hear what the residents had decided, they walked into a meeting of more than two hundred people assembled in the community church. One family alone offered to donate seventy-five acres of land, and everywhere the women turned others stepped forward to press promissory notes into their hands for labor, supplies, tools, and more. The Appalachian people, they quickly discovered, were hungry for classrooms and teachers and held education in high regard.

In 1925 builders turned the first shovelful of dirt for the school that would be named after Olive's late husband. The John C. Campbell Folk School soon opened on acres of hilly terrain and lush meadows that nestled in a valley between the mountains. In its early days most students who attended the school came to learn more about traditional southern Appalachian arts, crafts, and agricultural practices, but as the years went by, the world began to change, and the school continues to change and adapt with it, introducing new teachers who bring a variety of crafts, materials, and skills from other, often distant, cultures.[5]

Today, more than eighty years since its humble beginnings, the Folk School attracts students from across the United States and abroad, and it's easy to understand why. As our society becomes increasingly technology oriented, much of the work we do exists only in cyberspace. Aside from occasionally printing a corporate report or sales receipt, there isn't a lot of material substance to what most of us do each day. We don't cut and stitch the beautiful quilts that cover our beds; they arrive packaged in plastic bags from the mall. We don't shape a vase from clay to hold fresh-cut flowers from our yard; the vase and the blossoms are purchased from a florist. Real craftsmen are disappearing, displaced by fast, cheap production methods, and few of us work with our hands anymore.

Since I admire handiwork and skilled craftsmanship, I was ripe for the picking, so to speak, when one of the Folk School's glossy color catalogs arrived in my mailbox one morning, carrying a description about a class on canning and preserving produce from the garden.

That year record levels of rainfall had turned the red clay in my garden into a sticky muck that kept me from planting; yet over the winter we'd eaten almost all the pickles, relishes, and fruit preserves we'd "put up" the previous year.

Our supply of homegrown goodies was shrinking. One look at the catalog and my mouth watered at the thought of feasting on meaty, ripe tomatoes, tender snap beans, and fresh figs that I could process to see us through the coming winter.

With a few days of vacation to enjoy, I enrolled in the cooking and canning class at the Folk School. "Fill your pantry with glistening, brightly-colored jars," the catalog read, and my head swam with visions of my kitchen windowsill lined with batches of apple jam, apricot-honey mustard, and tomato salsa. A hint that the students might also come away with pints of slow-roasted pears packed in honey-sweetened syrup sealed the deal.

Soon I was driving along the winding road toward Brasstown, a small village at the western edge of the state, with three cases of empty glass canning jars clattering in my back seat. I knew I'd have to work for my goodies; the supply list sent by the school told me to bring an apron and a hat with a brim, sure signs that we'd be going into the school's big garden to pick our own fresh fruits and veggies, along with the glass jars and lids. As I drove onto the grounds, I hoped I could hold my own in the culinary classroom once we started chopping, simmering, and processing, especially if my classmates turned out to be gourmet chefs.

"This is like a camp for adults," said Jan Davidson, the school's director, as he cheerfully welcomed all the new students on my first morning there. We gathered early, at 7:45 a.m., for a Danish custom of starting the day with music and fellowship known as Morningsong. Jan told us about the Campbells, the school's founders, but assured us that nothing we'd experience would involve heavy educational theories or impossibly serious idealism.

The Folk School, Jan told us, was all about learning for the sheer love of learning, and students loved its classes because they were real and down-to-earth. "[The school] ain't 'virtual,'" he added, laughing, "and you can't just watch. It is hands-on and all senses engaged, and it's as deeply intellectual as you care to make it."

When a farm bell clanged, calling us to the dining hall, we hurried off to take our places at long wooden tables. After a song and quick devotional, we shared our meal family-style, passing platters of scrambled eggs and fresh-baked brown bread. Jan urged us to sit with a different group every time we met for a meal, since getting to know different people from different walks of life is a big part of the school's purpose.

After breakfast I joined my new classmates in the cooking studio, which was equipped with multiple stovetops and sinks, food processors and blenders, and plenty of saucepans and maple spoons hand-carved by woodworking students.

I was amazed to meet the diverse group of people who had come for the same thing I had: the sheer pleasure of doing something useful and productive with one's hands. Two men who had never cooked before had bravely signed up to learn canning after their wives took off to learn to play the dulcimer on another part of the campus.

For our first cooking task, learning how to prepare bread and butter pickles, I paired off with one of the men, who turned out to be the friendly, veteran commander of a nuclear submarine, the *USS Daniel Boone*. Later I chopped and sliced with Rich, the other man in the group and the commander's fellow parishioner from St. Peter's Episcopal Church in Fernandino Beach, Florida. Still later I'd rotate through cooking partners that included a stay-at-home mom; an accomplished seamstress; and a seventy-nine-year-old retired baseball fan from New York City, a woman who had already attended many classes at the school over the years to improve her tinsmithing work. Together we were going to can dilly beans spiked with cayenne peppers, whip up luscious peach-mango chutney with crystallized ginger, and preserve salsa with spicy green onions and scarlet peppers.

We began by grabbing hats and heading for the school's organic garden. Summer had turned the garden into a kaleidoscope of colors: pink and purple-blue morning glories, dark green chard, and ruby tomatoes. Cucumbers and beans hid in a tangle of vines. Our instructor, Jan's wife, Nanette, let us pluck ripe cherry tomatoes from the vine for a snack, an old-timey sweet variety known as Matt's Wild Cherry. Each bite tasted like a burst of sugar in my mouth, and soon we were pocketing extras to dry for seeds.

Back in the studio, we learned new skills and whipped up new recipes each day, always preparing enough canned goods so that each student would have plenty of pepper relish, bean chutney, Moroccan lemons, and apricot mustard to take home at the end of our workweek. We pressed raspberries into a ruby pulp for jam, sauntered down the road for the last of the summer's tart green apples, and drove to a local farmers's market to buy fat onions and fresh spices like turmeric and dill. I wondered idly, as we boiled pots of vinegary brine for pickles, if we were also pickling a class of student poets one flight up from our kitchen studio.

In my spare time I wandered around the 360-acre campus, sticking my nose into various classrooms and workshops to check out other students' work in progress: a menagerie of stuffed, felted bears in the fiber arts building; fireplace tools being forged in the blacksmithing barn; and rows of jars and bowls awaiting a turn in the pottery studio's kiln. There were no grades, no critiques, and no peer panels to judge the Shaker cabinet or dim sum dumplings being made in other classes; no one laughed at a beginning knitter's lopsided socks or an artist's rough sketches.

After dinner one evening I stood in a sprinkle of light rain to watch an instructor demonstrate chair making. As the teacher straddled an old-style shaving horse, a kind of combination vice and workbench, he explained that he was teaching his students how to utilize tools and techniques from the 1860s to the 1890s so that they could turn their red oak lumber into traditional mountain rocking chairs without ever touching a power tool or a sheet of modern sandpaper.

Other students were working late in the basketry studio, ripping white oak logs into splits, which are thin strips that must be soaked in water to make them pliable enough for weaving. Clearly this old craft wasn't for weaklings; separating the wood took a lot of upper body strength and a pair of strong hands. I stepped inside the room to heft a finished basket with leather handles, hoping to purchase it, until its maker, a tired-looking woman, spotted me. She lifted her apron to wipe her sweaty face and brushed her stray hair out of her eyes. "Not for sale," she said, noticing my interest. She opened her hands to show me weeping blisters on both red palms. Smiling, she added, "Not for sale at any price."

As it turned out, her raw hands had a story to tell. She was recently widowed, the woman went on to tell me, and to deal with her grief and loss, she'd taken a leave from her job to come to the mountains to rest and find peace. Every day, she explained, she deliberately wore herself out, splitting the oak strips and wrestling them into forms for her basket. The fatigue and blisters were helping distract her from her terrible emotional pain. Using her hands was also helping her gain confidence, she said, since she knew she would have to learn new tasks that lay ahead in her days alone, like managing a checkbook, buying her car tags, negotiating insurance, and even climbing a tall ladder to change a burned-out light fixture in her garage.

She reminded me of Jacob, who wrestled one night with a being who might have been an angel or God himself; the

Scriptures refer first to a "man," but later we are told that Jacob "struggled with God" (Gen. 32:28).

Jacob, whose own hands were probably strong and muscled from years of hard manual labor, held the stranger in his grasp until he was given a blessing. Even though Jacob was left with a permanent limp from the struggle, at last he was able to say, "I have been delivered" (Gen. 32:30). There was something about that encounter, something about literally using his hands and grappling with God in a physical way, that finally allowed Jacob to receive God's grace, even though it did not come easily. Many of us have experienced God in the same way; we've had to wrestle with what we believed, and with who God really is, to push through our doubts or fears and come out victorious on the other side.

Physical struggles and manual labor. Using our hands. Everywhere I looked that week I saw hands at work—sculpting, sewing, hammering, and painting. Some were coated with slick clay from potter's wheels or burned from hot soldering irons used to piece together kaleidoscopes and stained glass windows. Some hands moved like blurs as fuzzy socks formed on knitting needles; others strummed banjo strings, bound leather journals, or kneaded loaves of elastic dough for crusty baked bread. There were hands that moved with ease and those that fumbled with new and awkward tasks, but as I watched, I realized what grace it is to have work for our hands, and I marveled at how good and satisfying physical labor can be.

In Deuteronomy, Moses talked about work when he spoke to the Israelites near the end of their forty-year journey through the desert. As he stood on the plains near the Jordan River in Moab, he reminded the younger generation, the one that would finally enter the Promised Land, that there was only one true God, and that blessings flowed when they obeyed his words.

Moses urged the people to soften their hearts. "Then you will again obey Him and follow all His commands I am giving you today. The LORD your God will make you prosper abundantly in all the work of your hands" (Deut. 30:8–9).

I'm aware, when I read this verse, that the Scripture isn't promising material abundance just because we obey, but I like what this does promise, which is a kind of synergy. We are to do our work, using whatever gifts we are given—and we all have gifts—and God will do his part. He will provide what we need, whether it's distraction from grief or food for the table, or just the very real joy of seeing something take shape and form and substance in our hands.

In a society stripped of physical contact, often we encounter each other only by e-mail and cell phone. However, carving a chunk of turpentine-scented pine with a knife that fits neatly into your palm or combing your fingers through a hank of silky yarn invites us to draw closer to the One who created the metal that goes into the tool and the sheep that gives the wool.

Watch a calligrapher draw his pen and ink across a rough page as he traces out the alphabet, and consider the patience and practice required to achieve that beautiful script. Then think, when a handicraft requires such effort and skill, how wondrously and intricately God has made us, his children, with his hands and in his image. The pleasure we find in our work echoes, in the most rudimentary way, the pleasure God takes in us, his creation. He is the ultimate Artist and Craftsman. It takes a mighty God to shape us from nothing more than breath and dust, and realizing that is a humbling thing. "I will praise You," says Psalm 139:14, "because I have been remarkably and wonderfully made."

In another psalm the writer entreated God to "establish for us the work of our hands," (Ps. 90:17) repeating for emphasis, "establish the work of our hands!" His plea was our permission to ask God to bless whatever we make, do, or create through our labor.

All work is a holy thing and a blessing, no matter whether we spend our days in office cubicles or behind cash registers; whether we reel crab pots onto a fishing boat, watch children in a day care center, or trade futures on the floor of the New York Stock Exchange.

God honors hard, authentic work. Even when we're inclined to groan when the alarm clock goes off or count the days until we can retire, we know in our hearts that having work to do is a gift. When we do our tasks with appreciation to the Giver, we are doubly blessed.

So that no one forgets its reason for being, the motto for the Folk School is carved into one of the old wooden barns on its land. The words read "I Sing behind the Plow," and they are there to remind students that no matter what they do with their hands, hearts, or heads, pleasure and satisfaction are to be found in labor. The motto is an irresistible call to work with joy, even if, as Davidson says, nowadays most of us wind up singing behind a computer screen.

For one week in the mountains, I canned and pickled and processed the fruits and vegetables from the garden at the Campbell Folk School, and when my classes were over, I packed up my glass jars, filled with bright green beans, fragrant pears, and confetti-colored relish, and stowed them in the trunk of my car. Before I drove home, I decided to take one last, quick stroll around the campus. The path I chose, lined with daylilies, bordered a field overgrown with tall grass.

Motto notwithstanding, I hadn't seen anyone plowing or even mowing since I'd arrived, but as I walked along, I saw some of the staff drive up with a trailer in tow, preparing to cut the field. One man hopped onto a riding mower and cranked it, filling the air with a noisy snarl. I turned around and headed back to my car, eager to duck the swirl of dust and grass the machine was sure to kick up.

That's when I saw her.

One of the workers on the cutting crew was a slender girl, just a teenager, wielding a gas-powered weed whacker. She looked a lot like the Goth kids who hang around our local coffee shop, clad in her black shirt, black jeans, and stout black boots.

Even her chin-length hair was dyed a matte ebony and snipped in short, fierce spikes. I caught a flash of sunlight glint off the multiple silver studs she wore in her ears and nose.

Soon more power tools were ringing in my ears, so I picked up my pace, trying to avoid the sting of debris the mower was starting to sling in my direction. But even with the noise around me, as I passed the girl on the path, the sound I heard was unmistakable. Over the whine of the weed whacker, as she leaned into the prickly weeds and high grass that covered the overgrown field, I caught the sound of her high, clear voice. She was singing.

Flying with Angels

Love one another.

—John 13:34

T hink you'd recognize an angel if you saw one? According to the Bible, God's heavenly messengers have appeared in different forms to different people throughout the ages. Sometimes they've even been invisible, as Elisha's servant discovered during a battle with the Arameans, when God opened his eyes to reveal a host of previously unseen horses and chariots fighting on Israel's side. But most of the time, we imagine that angels look the way they've been portrayed in popular culture—that is, as beautiful beings with halos and fluffy white wings.

You remember. In 1996 actor John Travolta, who once strutted the streets of New York City in the film *Saturday Night Fever*, turned in his white disco suit for a trench coat to hide his angel wings in the movie *Michael* (he also managed a mean boogie to "Chain of Fools" without dropping a single feather). A decade or so before that, a rash of "angel mania" broke out around the country when the celestial spirits started turning up everywhere, from TV shows like *Touched by an Angel* with actress Della Reese, to director Michael Landon's *Highway to Heaven*, and in coffee-table books, songs, wall art, and greeting cards. Most of those angels sported ethereal accessories too.

Of course, nobody knows whether angels look like handsome Travolta or motherly Reese or even the cheeky cherubs in Renaissance paintings; in some verses in the Bible, they suddenly and simply appear as male messengers dressed in snowy-white robes. They can even look like the rest of us, because some people, the Bible says, have encountered angels without recognizing them. We also know that angels can show up in a blaze of glory when they have great news to announce, as the angels did at Jesus' birth and again at his resurrection. Other than that, your guess about their shape and form is as good as mine.

But ask Brody and Kristi Cole, and they'll tell you that they've met plenty of angels with wings—pilot's wings, that is.

Seven-year-old Brody and his mom, Kristi, have been flying with their special "angels," who are actually licensed pilots with privately owned planes, since Brody was just two. That's when the digestive problems that had been plaguing him were diagnosed as the result of a rare genetic mitochondrial disorder.

Nicknamed the "powerhouse" of the cells, "the mitochondria are the parts of the cells that make energy for your body," Kristi explains. Because Brody's don't function properly, they have caused multiple organ damage, leaving him in need of a triple transplant for a new stomach, small bowel, and pancreas.

In short, Brody, a handsome little guy who loves the Power Rangers and wearing his yellow rain boots, who lives with his mom and two older brothers in Georgia, can't eat anything by mouth, and that includes medicines that can only be taken orally. For the last five years, Brody has had to take all his nourishment and medication through IV tubes. That means he can't eat a candy bar or piece of toast, no eggs or rice or chicken. In fact, for those past five years, he's never been detached from his nutritional IV lines for more than six days at a stretch. Small wonder, then, that when you ask him what he'd like to do one day, when he grows up, Brody replies with something that would never occur to most of us. His dream, he says, is to eat a hot dog.

Brody's flesh-and-blood angels want to make that dream come true, along with a lot of other dreams Brody hasn't even had a chance to dream yet, and they're using their pilot's wings and planes to help. They are the men and women of Angel Flight of Georgia, a nonprofit organization based at Georgia's Peachtree-DeKalb Airport. These volunteer pilots and ground support staff help provide free transportation for Georgia residents who are ambulatory patients with legitimate and verifiable medical and financial needs. Similar charitable transportation agencies exist in other states around the United States. If you need help, or if you can give it, you can find these agencies listed on the Internet under a nationwide league of humanitarian flying groups called the Air Care Alliance.[6]

Brody qualifies for Angel Flight services because he can't travel on commercial planes. Most public airlines can't accommodate his IV tubes and pump, nor the forty-pound box of medications, fluids, and other supplies that Kristi has to keep close at hand for him. Traveling by car is a problem, too, because he and his mom would have to drive far to see the specialists he needs, who work at pediatric hospitals and clinics across the country.

When Brody had to visit a Pittsburgh specialist, the family endured a thirteen-hour car trip, Kristi explains, a journey that would be tough to pull off with any young child, even one in perfect health. Cost is another consideration. As fuel prices continue to soar, so does the price of an airline ticket. That's why an Angel Flight pilot ferries Brody and his mom to one of his regular checkups every three months. While the Pittsburgh hospital is one of only a handful of centers in the United States where nutritionists and pediatric specialists can help Brody right now, it looks as if he'll have to travel to Seattle—all the way across the country from his Georgia home—when his transplant finally comes through.

Brody was originally on a waiting list to replace all three of his damaged organs, but recently, Kristi says, the wait has become too long. A suitable donor would have to be a child of approximately his same size and age, and such donors are few and far between. Time is a factor in Brody's case, too, so as of this writing, his doctors have opted to list him only for the small bowel transplant. They hope that replacing even that one organ would open the door for giving Brody certain medications that are available right now only in oral form, meds that could help control some of his other issues, such as his high blood pressure and unstable autonomic functions.

Angel Flight pilots can help until a transplant becomes available—and no one can predict when that might be, so Kristi keeps her cell phone on at all times, for the emergency call that everyone is praying for. But when Brody is finally summoned for the transplant at a pediatric hospital, he'll have to go via air ambulance with a trained medical crew who can keep him stable.

Brody has already flown so much, he should have his own set of wings. He's a fearless little guy who loves to look out the windows at the passing scenery and listen to the radio trans- missions when a pilot lets him don a pair of headphones. He can even handle making connections, the bane of every air traveler's existence; because these small planes usually can't carry enough fuel to take patients long distances, families frequently have to transfer from one volunteer flight to another. It's a necessary stop and one that often prolongs an already difficult and tiring trip, but Kristi praises the staff and crew, who frequently go the extra mile and help arrange a taxi or ride to the hospital after the family lands.

Arrangements like these take a lot of behind-the-scenes work and planning, but even the approximately eight hundred volunteer pilots of Angel Flight of Georgia aren't always enough. Retiree Mack Secord, who joined the organization in 1985 after putting in twenty-two years with the U.S. Air Force, warns that we shouldn't be fooled by the large number of pilots that make up the network.

"Eight hundred sounds like a lot," Mack says, but "I've seen our scheduling people call twenty-five or more pilots just to find one who's available." That's because many pilots work full-time jobs and may not be able to take time off to fly a compassionate trip. Planes that are down for maintenance or repair can also cause scheduling to back up.

Pilots don't just give generously of their time; they also spend a lot of their own money. "Pilots [who sign on with Angel Flight of Georgia] have to provide their own planes and fuel and pay all the expenses of a trip," Mack explains. His Cessna 182 burns about thirteen gallons of aviation gas (which is not the same as jet fuel) per hour, and while he's able to save money by filling up at a couple of small airfields he frequents, he says gas runs about six dollars a gallon at most places now. "It's hard to say what a pilot spends on average," Mack says. "Each flight depends on the length of the trip, the size of the plane, and so forth. But I'd say you'd spend an average of $500 to $700 a trip."

With all the time and costs involved, why does anyone go to this much trouble?

John Lauth, who assisted Angel Flight in the early '90s and started volunteering again in 2005, quotes a physician when he answers that question—a very old physician, in fact, named Luke. In Luke 12:48, Luke, quoting Jesus, said, "Much will be required of everyone who has been given much. And even more will be expected of the one who has been entrusted with more."

John believes this is true. He says he's been blessed as the founder and CEO of Courier Connection, a same-day delivery and transportation business in Atlanta, but it's clear that he sees his material success as a means to help others.

"How many cars can I drive?" John asks. "How many planes can I fly? It's simple really. I'm a steward, a manager of what I have. My plane, my income—they're not mine. For whatever reason I was blessed, I feel called to give back. If you've got it, give it. Share it."

These guys sound heroic, but don't bother trying to pin any halos on John or Mack or the other Angel Flight pilots. "We're not the heroes here," John says. "We just jump in a plane and take a little flight." He credits the volunteer ground staff for putting pilots and patients together and scheduling the necessary trips. Besides, "I want to be able to say that I did everything I could with the hand I was dealt," he adds. "The New Testament is like an instruction manual, in many ways, on how to do that.

Christ taught us how to live, and to me, it's just asking myself what is the right thing to do."

Mack is equally self-effacing and tries to deflect praise. "There are few things in life that let you indulge your passion while you help other people. Flying is my passion," he says. But he hasn't fooled anybody. In September 2009 the National Aeronautic Association, in Washington, D.C., invited Mack to the Lyndon B. Johnson Room of the U.S. Senate, where it honored him with its Public Benefit Flying Awards Distinguished Volunteer Pilot designation, the most prestigious award for this kind of charitable work in the country. Back home in Georgia, a local TV station presented Mack with one of eleven annual sought-after Community Service Awards. "It's been a pretty good year," he admits with a soft chuckle.

Many Angel Flight volunteers are like John and Mack; since the organization took to the skies in 1983, its pilots, who also serve Alabama, Mississippi, Tennessee, the Carolinas, and a few parts of Florida, have completed more than two thousand missions for patients who range in age from newborns to eighty-seven-year-old seniors. More than one thousand volunteers serve in Georgia as pilots and ground staff, who are lovingly known as Earth Angels, with the support of only a handful of paid employees.

In Jesus' time—as in ours—it wasn't always easy to find someone who was willing to give his time to others. That's why we remember the parable of the Good Samaritan. In the story an expert in Jewish law asked Jesus what he had to do to have eternal life.

Jesus threw the question right back in the man's lap. "You know the law," Jesus said, "so you tell me." The man began to recite, as if from memory, that believers were to "Love the Lord your God with all your heart, with all your soul, with all your strength, and with all your mind; and your neighbor as yourself" (Luke 10:27).

"That's right," Jesus agreed, but the man wouldn't let it drop. He continued to press Jesus, probably hoping he could wiggle out of being asked to serve in some way that would prove difficult or inconvenient.

"Neighbor?" the expert in Jewish law repeated. "What neighbor? I don't see anybody here. Who is this person I'm supposed to love?"

As if he didn't know.

That was when Jesus spoke to the man's heart. Once upon a time, he said, a man traveling along the road ran into serious trouble. He fell into the hands of robbers who beat him up and left him crumpled on the ground. Several people walked right by him that day and saw how much he needed help, but they didn't make time to stop and give aid. They stepped over him, thinking of their dinners cooling on the table at home, their business partners waiting to start a meeting, or their kids whining to be picked up for soccer practice. Helping wasn't convenient, and besides, who was this beat-up guy in the gutter? He looked dirty and might have some disease. No, he wasn't their neighbor or relative or friend, or he wouldn't look so bad and act so needy. They kept going.

Then a man from Samaria came by. When he saw the man, he was moved to interrupt his journey. He gave no thought to whatever differences might separate them; he simply stopped to help, and, the Bible tells us "had compassion" (Luke 10:33). He lifted the man and put him on "his own animal" (Luke 10:34) to move the beaten man to safety at a nearby inn. When the Samaritan was ready to resume his journey, he took coins from his pocket and pressed them into the innkeeper's hand, urging him to keep a record of any expenses. "I'll reimburse you for anything else that's needed," the man promised the innkeeper. Surely it isn't a coincidence that in some translations, the good "Samaritan" is called the good "neighbor."

"Now that you've heard my story," Jesus then told the expert in the law, "you tell me: Who acted like a neighbor?"

"The one who showed mercy" (Luke 10:37), the expert was forced to admit.

"Yes," Jesus said, "now go on your way and do likewise to someone else." Let compassion move you to love someone enough to give of yourself, your time, and your gifts, even if it's a sacrifice to you, and in so doing, you will obey God and honor him. "Don't neglect to do good and to share, for God is pleased with such sacrifices" (Heb. 13:16).

John, Mack, other pilots, and Earth Angels don't like to

make a big deal about the service they render. They insist that they're not doing that much, after all, that they're just small cogs in a big machine that works to aid Brody and others like him. They might even insist that patients like Brody literally are their "neighbors," because they live in the same or adjoining states.

But there's more than convenience or physical proximity going on here. The love of Jesus crosses all borders and is never earthbound. When it's shared from one heart to another, it's beautiful to see, even if you do have to pretend a little when it comes to halos and wings on his servants.

"I can't imagine not having faith," Kristi says, as she, Brody, and their family wait for the transplant they hope comes soon. "It gives me strength."

While they wait, Kristi has learned to take one day at a time. "We enjoy the day, because we know there's a bigger picture." When I last spoke to her, by phone, she, Brody, and his brothers were spending the afternoon around the kitchen table, playing a board game and having a great time; I could hear them laughing and chattering in the background. "We don't take things for granted," she says.

Kristi says she's even been able to experience God's grace and mercy through Brody's health issues. "I've gotten the ability to see even ordinary life as a blessing," she says, "even when I don't know what tomorrow holds or next week. I've seen the goodness in other people. When you turn on the radio, the news is all bad. But we don't even know most of the people who've sent letters to Brody or knitted prayer cloths or donated at fundraisers. Financially they don't have a lot, yet they give like they do. I've met people I never would have had the opportunity to meet."

Early in 2009 Brody suffered a stroke. It was one of those little mercies, that before he recovered his ability to speak, he was at least able to sing. One evening after he'd improved, Brody and Kristi went to a gospel sing at their church, and Kristi sent me the lyrics he planned to warble. They're from a song called "Hold On," and the words seem to describe the Coles' take on life:

Hold on . . . just a little bit longer,
Even though the skies above you are so gray.
Jesus, He will deliver you,
Who knows the sun may shine on you today![7]

The Son really does shine through the lives of those who care enough to make a difference. Their generosity of spirit is a sweet mercy.

"Let brotherly love continue," as the Scriptures say (Heb. 13:1). God has sent his angels to minister to us throughout the ages, as he sent the mysterious fourth "man" into the fiery furnace to rescue Shadrach, Meshach, and Abednego from King Nebuchadnezzar. Angels showed up to whisk Lot and his family away from Sodom and Gomorrah before God destroyed those cities. They've also appeared to deliver good news, issue warnings, and even minister to Jesus himself during his temptation in the desert.

God also sends us to each other, so you never know. Like John Travolta, maybe you should keep a trench coat at hand if you get up one morning and feel a call to help someone. You might discover a pair of wings you never knew you had; you might find out you can be someone's angel too.

Before this manuscript went to press, Brody Cole's earthly struggles came to a close. The doctors and nurses who cared for him, his Angel Flight helpers and supporters, and his grieving family and friends gathered at services and memorials to say good-bye to a special child who made every life he touched richer, deeper, and better. In spite of our sadness at saying good-bye for a while, Brody left us with a legacy of hope, because he showed us how to be happy, and how to love one another, even when we're in pain, exhausted, or uncertain about the future. Once we thought we could serve as earthly angels, ministering to him. Little did we know that all along, Brody was ministering to us.

Angel Flight is a nonprofit 501(c)(3) organization dedicated to helping patients who travel from, to, or through the states of Georgia, Alabama, Mississippi, Tennessee, and the Carolinas. If you can help, there are many ways for individuals or businesses to be involved. You don't need a pilot's license; Angel Flight can use Earth Angels, too, volunteers who work in its offices, assist with fund-raisers, write grant applications, arrange flight schedules, make scrapbooks, and much more. To request help from Angel Flight of Georgia or to earn a halo of your own, visit www.angelflightsoars.org. For information on other compassionate flight agencies that serve the rest of the United States, visit http://www.aircareall.org.

Drinking from the Spring

The LORD will always lead you, satisfy you in a parched land, and strengthen your bones. You will be like a watered garden and like a spring whose waters never run dry.

—Isaiah 58:11

I'm standing at the trailhead, listening for the rush of the Rio Grande in the gorge below, breathing in the spicy scents of pinyon and juniper, when the llamas start to hum. Stuart Wilde, the intrepid guide leading the tour I'm on,[8] rips open a big nylon bag with his pocket knife and gestures to the dozen or so tourists who have signed up for this half-day trek. "Dig in," he urges, grinning, and we gather round to plunge our hands into a mixture of sweet feed oats and other grains.

One of the llamas, a handsome, cream-colored male named Azul, is kneeling, camel-like, beside Stuart's truck, so I stoop to offer him the snack and am rewarded with the unexpected delight of feeling his warm nose nuzzle my fingers. With his soft, fuzzy ears, Bugs Bunny buck teeth, and gentle disposition, he reminds me of an overgrown white rabbit. He munches as he watches me with one chocolate-brown eye and then swivels his head to reveal a sky-blue eye on the other side.

"Azul was my first llama," says Stuart, a passionate naturalist and New York native who ditched an unsatisfying city life to open a wilderness adventures business back in 1992. When Azul stands up, Stuart stuffs large water jugs, sandwiches, and fruit for our lunch into a satchel fastened over the llama's strong back, then turns and does the same with the other half dozen animals that will travel with us for the next few hours. "We've spent tens of thousands of hours and miles together over the last eighteen years," Stuart says, patting Azul. "He's getting close to retirement, but he still likes to come out and do this."

That sounds good to me. Azul looks like a wise and laid-back kind of guy, both desirable traits when you're choosing a hiking companion for a steep descent like this one, a switchback trail studded with sharp rocks and slippery gravel that begins in the Wild River National Recreation Area of New Mexico, about thirty-five miles north of Taos. But before I can take hold of Azul's lead and claim him for myself, another hiker in the group starts loading gear into the llama's pack from the other side. It's like having somebody jump into a cab you had whistled to the curb.

No matter. Stuart separates us anyway, assigning two hikers per animal, and passes me a bright red line attached to Zephyr, a young black llama that he describes as the feisty teenager of the herd. I look at Zephyr and he looks at me, both of us unsure of what we're getting into.

Not that we're going to ride the llamas. These are pack animals, not transportation, but still, I'm not sure that saucy Zephyr will cooperate with a hiking novice like me as willingly as the more experienced Azul would have. Zephyr eyeballs me as if he's not too crazy about his partner, either, but neither of us has an alternative at the moment. "Ready to go?" Stuart asks. He takes a long pull of water from his bottle before we begin.

We're all going to need water soon. It's only about a mile from the trailhead to the bottom of the canyon, some eight hundred feet from rim to river, but it's blazing hot at the top of the gorge and this moderate-to-difficult hike begins at an elevation several thousand feet higher than I'm used to back home. That means my lungs are soon pumping like a fireplace bellows, but no matter how I gasp, throughout the climb, I will feel as if I'm getting about half the usual amount of air.

Zephyr, on the other hand, is young, energetic, and primed for our outing. Gingerly I stroke the wiry hair on his neck. He may look fluffy, but his hair isn't soft like a cat's or dog's, and what I'd always heard, Stuart admits, is true. Llamas spit. It's a "guy thing," he explains, a dominance behavior between males, and something his nicely trained animals seldom do. Nevertheless I stay out of the line of fire, which means walking slightly behind or in front of Zephyr. Llamas are accustomed to walking single file anyway, in follow-the-leader style, and they like it that way.

Soon my buddy Zep and two other llamas, K2 and Domino, take up Azul's soft hum as we walk along. It's a nasally little sound the animals use to communicate with each other and express everything from curiosity to nervousness. "It's like their whistle as they walk through the woods," Stuart says. "Llamas are prey animals, and they're nervous by nature." He tells our group to think about it; llamas don't have strong natural defenses, so they have to stay alert and ready to run. "When you're food for somebody else, you're never all that settled." He also tells the group that in the last twenty-five years, there has been a renewed interest in these gentle, intelligent llamas, which were once domesticated by the Incas. When the Inca civilization fell, the animals almost became extinct, but now breeders in the United States are once again raising them as hiking companions and pets, and even—brace yourself—as a food source, another possible reason for all that nervous humming.

But aside from their soft murmurs, our little llamas prove to be rather quiet creatures, which has earned them the name "yyamas," or silent brothers, among the indigenous people of the Andean highlands.[9] They're actually part of the camelid family—think camels without humps—and they've been used in

South America as beasts of burden and as a source of wool and fiber for more than six thousand years.

As we descend, we hit rough patches on the trail. Pebbles roll under my feet, making me slip, and occasionally we're forced to pick our way over sharp outcroppings of rocks. The sun moves high above us in the sky, baking the ground underfoot, and soon we're all plucking our water bottles out of their pouches and downing big gulps. I polish off my bottle and Stewart gives me a quick refill from one of the jugs in Azul's pack, but before long, I've knocked that one back too. Soon we're all refilling and chugging water.

Within an hour or so, we reach the river. It's a hard hike for humans who are bumble-footed and unacclimated to the elevation, like me, but the hilly terrain is no challenge for our four-footed companions, who have split toes that give them sure footing. The animals literally leave a small footprint on the earth, and the priciest hiking boots can't match these furry mountaineers when it comes to stability and agility.

A self-taught naturalist and field ecologist, Stuart stops from time to time to talk about the scenery, and some of us take a break to uncap our water bottles as he gestures around. We're all getting sweaty and some, like me, are already tiring. But our lunch stop is just minutes ahead, Stuart assures us, so we forge on.

Thankfully the air begins to cool as we descend lower and lower, and soon we're able to glimpse the sun-spangled river. Near the bottom of the gorge, we loop our leads over tree branches and stop to rest in the shade at beautiful Big Arsenic Spring. Crystal-clear water bubbles out of its volcanic rocks, filling a pool fringed by lush ferns and studded with mossy boulders. It's hard to resist dipping my hands (or at least an empty water bottle) into the water, but Stewart asks us to refrain, so we don't disturb its pristine beauty. Instead, he cuts a sprig of watercress that's growing around the spring and passes it to us to sample. One nibble leaves my tongue stinging with a spicy bite like horseradish. We keep guzzling water from the supply he has brought along as Zephyr, Azul, and the other llamas snack, using their split lips like little spoons, on fresh-fallen pine needles and the leaves they rip from surrounding trees.

Water, water, water. Now I understand why Stuart put so many extra containers in the llamas' packs. The heat of the day combined with the physical exertion and high altitude has given me a powerful thirst, like everyone else on this excursion. I'm grateful we're sitting at the foot of the spring, even if we're not supposed to drink directly from it. At least the llamas are doing fine—they're kin to camels, remember, and have a high tolerance to thirst.

It's easy, from this trip, to understand how a source of clean, constantly flowing water like a well or spring has been a prized possession since ancient times. Achsah, the daughter of Caleb, asked for such a gift in the Old Testament days. Born during the years that the Israelites wandered through the desert, Achsah was given by her father in marriage to Othniel, a warrior. She persuaded her new husband to ask Caleb for a field, so the just-married couple could grow crops and establish a home, and Caleb, apparently a doting father, granted her wish. Then Achsah decided she needed something else from her dad: "'Give me a blessing. Since you have given me land in the Negev, give me springs of water also.' So Caleb gave her both the upper and lower springs" (Judg. 1:15).

"Give me a blessing," Achsah pleaded. "Give me water." Her father complied.

Achsah's story must be significant because it appears twice in the Bible, in the book of Joshua and again in Judges. Maybe it's repeated because water is the equivalent of wealth in a desert land, vital to the health and very survival of fields, animals, and people. But as the late English pastor Charles Haddon Spurgeon speculated in one of his Victorian-era sermons, Achsah's request has something to teach us besides the value of springs in dry places. Her story is in the Scriptures to encourage all of us to go to our heavenly Father and ask for what we need, just as Achsah went to her earthly father.

Even the way Achsah approached her father is a model for how we are to go before the throne. Achsah, Spurgeon said, rode on an ass when she went to see Caleb, which would have been the customary way for a woman to travel in that time. When Achsah spotted her father, she immediately dismounted, "a token of great and deep respect, just as Rebecca, when she saw Isaac, alighted from the camel," Spurgeon wrote.[10] We're to make our requests in humility and love, too, with hearts that are ready to accept our Father's will, whatever it may be.

We have a New Testament story about water and a woman too. When Jesus passed through Samaria on his way from Jerusalem to Galilee, tired from his trip, he stopped at a well on the edge of town to rest while his disciples went to find food for a meal. As he sat alone, a Samaritan woman came to fill her water jug. In this story it wasn't a woman who asked for water, as Achsah did, but Jesus himself.

The woman was surprised when Jesus spoke to her. A Jew acknowledging a Samaritan? Their people were longtime enemies, and this encounter was out of the ordinary. I can imagine the woman arching her eyebrows and frowning in disbelief. "You want something from me?" she said in reply. "You've got to be kidding. I'm supposed to fetch a drink of water for you?"

Jesus may have smiled, knowing that he was about to give her a blessing, not the other way around. "If you knew the gift of God, and who is saying to you, 'Give Me a drink,' you would ask Him, and He would give you living water," Jesus replied (John 4:10).

"Wait a minute," the woman said, astounded. "You don't even have a bucket, and this is a deep, deep well. How are you going to get any water?" She didn't realize that Jesus didn't have to fetch the water because he *was* the water.

Her well might have satisfied a person's thirst for a while,

Jesus explained, but any relief he found wouldn't last. *He* could satisfy someone's thirst forever. "In fact, the water I will give him will become a well of water springing up within him for eternal life" (John 4:14). The woman stood before him, amazed, letting her water jug slip to the ground.

One of the wonderful things about this story is how Jesus reached out to an ordinary woman with his extraordinary gift. Not far away her village was probably home to at least a few educated men or priests, scholars who could have shared this important message with others in carefully chosen words and put it into a learned context. Their testimony would have given weight to Jesus' teachings, because the other townspeople would hold the scholars in high esteem.

But Jesus wasn't interested in going through the higher-ups. He came to share himself, personally, with those the world didn't know or even notice. In this instance he offered his living water to a sinful woman who would have been considered an outcast among her people because of her adultery.

When Jesus mentioned the many men with whom the woman had lived, and the one she was currently living with out of wedlock, she first thought she'd encountered a prophet. Then he revealed himself as the Messiah, and she believed, running into town, her empty jug forgotten, to spread the word that the promised One had come at last.

Later that afternoon our group left Big Arsenic Spring and made one last push to the powerful and beautiful Rio Grande at the bottom of the gorge. Again we let our llamas rest while we sat on rocks that jutted out over the water and pulled off our sweaty socks and shoes to dangle our feet in the cold river. I dunked my hat and poured scoop after scoop of water over my head, reveling in the refreshment, blinking as water streamed into my dry, dusty eyes.

When the llamas were ready, we regrouped for the challenging hike back up the trail to the Wild River recreation area. Our view of the river vanished as we climbed higher and higher into thick stands of trees, and soon the sound of the rushing water disappeared. The sun beat down on us again, forcing us to pull out handkerchiefs to wipe our sweaty faces and reach once more for something to slake our thirst.

Our path back to the canyon's rim was clearly marked by hikers and llamas that had gone before us, and eventually we emerged at the trailhead, exhausted but exhilarated by the day. The llamas knelt down again in the shade to receive another snack from Stuart, and the rest of us piled into our cars and cranked up the air conditioning, suddenly very grateful for modern conveniences.

Not all journeys end so well. Without an expert guide, it would be easy to stray into the wilderness and get lost. Without enough water to drink, you could perish on your way. Amazing how a simple cup of water can restore your health and energy. Amazing how the right kind of Water can restore your very soul.

A few years ago I made a wonderful new friend at church. My buddy Tom, at seventy-some years old, is probably the world's biggest fan of the University of Georgia's football team, the Bulldogs. He wears the team colors, red and black, on his jackets, shirts, pants, and hats; he drives a shiny red car and an older red pickup truck. Call his house, and you'll hear the Georgia fight song when his answering machine picks up. When the Bulldogs happen to lose a game—and he'd tell you that's rare—he wears a black armband to church to signify that he's in mourning. There's even a snarling Georgia bulldog printed on the back of his church name tag. (I know because I put it there as a favor to him.)

Tom is your go-to guy when you want someone to don a silly wig and host the church talent show—dressed up as Donald Trump. He teaches a Sunday school class and serves as an elder; mans the grill at our barbecues and picnics; has taught our youth for many years; mentors young members (so lovingly and easily that they usually don't realize he's even doing it); and leads the charge to bring back members who've slipped away or just plain walked away from our congregation for whatever reason. He plays guitar, loves Batman movies, and works as a volunteer in our church office, writing notes to shut-ins, answering the phones, and even bringing in breakfast biscuits when the early morning employees in the church haven't had time to grab a bite at home.

I hope I'm painting a picture of an outgoing, fun-loving man who is as devoted to his brothers and sisters in Christ as he is to the Lord himself.

A couple of years ago Tom suffered a blow. His dear wife, Betty, passed away after a long and brave struggle with complications from multiple sclerosis. He stayed faithfully at her side through her last hospitalization, joined by our interim pastor, Tim, and friends and elders who came to sing, pray, and even entertain Betty with silly jokes until she slipped away.

Tom grieved hard for Betty, and those of us who loved them grieved to see his pain. Yet Tom did something most people of his age don't do. After a short rest, he rallied. He got back into his church work again, since he'd had to step away for a while to nurse Betty. Through the county school system, he found a little boy to mentor. (He also bought the child a Georgia Bulldogs cap, apparently thinking that while he was at it, he might as well grow another new fan.)

I love Tom because when I look at him, I see Jesus, and that makes him a powerful witness to others. His life is a sermon—a memorable, enduring one—because he has stuck with Jesus (he would say, "Jesus has stuck with me") through good times and bad.

Tom has drunk from the Living Water, and that has made all the difference.

After the woman at the well talked to Jesus, she left behind the jar she had for her well water, to run and tell others about the Living Water.

That's what happens when you meet Jesus and take him as your life's guide. You will jump in a swimming pool, dangle your feet in a river, run through the lawn sprinkler, or do whatever it takes to get completely soaked, utterly wet, totally immersed in that pure and precious flow. The Living Water has poured out through the ages; what grace, that it refreshes us still.

Mountain Time

*How beautiful on the mountains are the feet of
the herald, who proclaims peace, who brings news
of good things, who proclaims salvation, who says
to Zion, "Your God reigns!"*

—Isaiah 52:7

You can lose track of time when you're standing in the dark on top of a mountain, and I don't mean just the time of day. In the Great Smoky Mountains of Tennessee, as the morning's blue-gray mists curl up into the trees around you, it's easy to lose your orientation and sense of direction—easy, even to forget the high-tech age we're living in. There's a feeling of timelessness in these ancient hills.

I felt it as I stood high in the Smokies one day, shivering in the chill before dawn. In a nearby valley a flock of wild turkeys, hidden from sight by brush and trees, woke up to the new day and launched into a frenzy of loud gobbling. I stuffed my hands in my jeans pockets and threw the hood of my jacket over my head, trying to stay warm until the sun peeked over the distant hills and threw ribbons of orange and gold over the landscape.

While I waited, teeth chattering, I couldn't help wondering what it must have been like for the native Cherokees who once hunted game in these birches and hickories, or for the first settlers who arrived in the late 1700s, to hack clearings out of the dense woods to build their plain cabins and hog pens, humble churches, and split-rail fences. Life was hard back then, with heavy snows that fell each winter and temperatures that froze streams of drinking water into solid ice. Food supplies were uncertain, the soil was stony, and dangerous bears and snakes roamed the wilderness. And just imagine the isolation: medicines, supplies, and even neighbors were far away.

The people who hunted, built, and raised their families in these mountains are long gone, of course, nothing more than memories or stories in books.

While the whippoorwills sang in the scrub, I tried to capture the scene and a sense of the long-ago past with my camera before it was time to rejoin a dozen or so other photographers who'd traveled with me to catch the sunrise on the ridge. We were doing a workshop on digital photography,[11] and this was the first day we'd lugged our tripods and cameras into the field as our instructors Tom and Pat Cory taught us how to capture the brilliance of a sunrise against the blackness of the mountains. When we finished photographing from the ridge, we'd hop back into our rented vans and drive to other locations around this national park, where we'd practice shooting everything from pastoral landscapes to close-ups of moss and dainty wild violets.

Before we headed out for our next stop, Tom, a professional photographer whose own work has appeared in books and many popular magazines, reminded us to take time—speaking of time and timelessness—to enjoy the view. Experience, he said, had shown him that photographers—especially inexperienced ones like me—would spend way too much of that fleeting commodity obsessing over the complex settings on our cameras, until we wound up missing the beauty around us.

Tom's wife, Pat, an accomplished photographer and videographer in her own right, stood by to answer our technical questions while Tom discussed the artistry behind creating great nature and travel photography. The best images, he told us, would spring from a photographer's personal vision.

To be sure, this was inspirational stuff, but before I could convey my personal vision—honestly, before I could even figure out what my personal vision was—I had to keep stopping to remove my lens cap. *What a rookie*, I thought. Without a vision Proverbs says, the people perish. Without an uncapped lens, a photographer gets no picture.

Clearly Tom and Pat, along with two able field assistants, had their work cut out for them.

Not that I was a complete newbie. I'd been hacking away at this hobby since the mid-'60s, when my parents bought me an oh-so-cool Polaroid Swinger camera, complete with jaunty wrist strap, for the then extravagant sum of $19.95. It boasted an innovative type of film that pulled out of the camera and developed right before your eyes—imagine, film you didn't have to drop off at the local drugstore—and we marveled to see black and white images appear out of a swirl of chemicals on its glossy paper.

Much later I moved up to a manual 35mm SLR camera, only to flounder as soon as I opened its instruction book, which read like an alphabet soup of instructions about f-stops, ISO/ASA, DIN range, and AE-S. In frustration I eventually stowed my little camera in the closet.

Still, my urge to get behind the lens never disappeared, and when a friend offered to loan me a new ten-megapixel, fully loaded monster of a camera, I jumped at the opportunity. It had one terrific feature my old camera lacked: a fully automatic mode, which meant that if I couldn't figure out how to set its buttons and dials and flashes, it was smart enough to program itself.

But even a good digital camera doesn't necessarily translate into good images. Although I put the borrowed camera on automatic, essentially using it as a "point and shoot" device, my pictures had been as disappointing as ever. Shots of animals and birds came out boring and distant; landscapes felt flat. Portraits looked stiff and unnatural. I couldn't figure out what was wrong.

"Composition," Tom said, nodding, when I described my problem. He told me I needed to go for simplicity. "Photography is largely subtractive. It's improved by what you take away and leave out." At one stop on our excursion, he demonstrated by taking me to see a tiny wildflower that had sprouted on the forest floor. After removing a crisscrossed handful of pine needles that had fallen over its blue and purple petals, he told me to stand directly over the flower and shoot straight down into its yellow throat. When I was finished, he put each pine needle back in place, careful to leave the scene the way we found it. He was right. The uncluttered background made the flower pop out in my finished image, a burst of bright color on the ground.

It's about learning to look for the small things, Pat added as she watched over our shoulders. "I've seen people hop out of a car, take a picture, and leave. They don't see how the light changes during the day, or the colors, how the world changes so much all the time."

Pat's words reminded me of a play I had to read in my high school English class, a classic called *Our Town*. Scripted by American playwright Thornton Wilder, this bare-bones little play was designed to be presented without any background scenery, and with only a few simple stage props. Propelled by a plainspoken narrator known as the Stage Manager, the play has a universal feel, with a story that could happen anywhere, and characters who could pass for your next-door neighbors.

Over the course of the play, the Stage Manager introduces us—the readers or audience—to a bunch of average, everyday folks who live in a fictional community called Grover's Corners. Two of the young residents of the town, George and Emily, marry during one act, but tragedy strikes nine years later—in 1913, according to the time-frame of the play—and Emily dies unexpectedly in childbirth.

But Emily can't rest in death. She appears again, in spirit form, to converse with the Stage Manager and tell him how much she misses her family and friends. She was so young, she says plaintively, and she had so much to live for; she begs to be allowed to go back into the world, just for a little while. Although he warns her against it, eventually, the compassionate Stage Manager agrees to let her return home for one more day. But he urges her not to choose a day that has any special significance. Pick an ordinary one, he tells her.

Emily chooses to relive her twelfth birthday, thinking that it's a safe choice. How many of us, after all, could remember what we did on one long-ago birthday? Emily finds herself back in her bedroom that morning, smelling the breakfast her mother is making for the family as they wait for her to come downstairs. At the table Emily opens a gift from her mother, a dress that was sent "all the way from Boston." Her father and little brother also have packages for her.

Suddenly Emily realizes it's too much to handle, too much to bear. She's overcome with emotion, finally realizing how precious an ordinary day was while she was living it. The bacon and waffles smelled so fresh, and her mother was so loving and thoughtful to order the pretty dress. How did she fail to appreciate all these wonderful things when she had them?

"I'm ready to go back," Emily tells the Stage Manager. Her birthday proved to be packed with so much love, excitement, fun, and promise, that her heart is stricken. It's only then that she recognizes how much she missed while she was living.[12]

She chooses to end her visit and wait patiently until her loved ones join her one day in the afterlife. "Good-by, Grover's Corners . . . Mama and Papa," she says sadly as she leaves. "Good-by to clocks ticking . . . and Mama's sunflowers. And food and coffee. And new-ironed dresses and hot baths . . . and sleeping and waking up. Oh, earth, you're too wonderful for anybody to realize you. Do any human beings ever realize life while they live it—every, every minute?"

"No," the store manager tells her thoughtfully. "Saints and poets, maybe—they do some."

Yes, saints and poets do get it, at least sometimes, but for the rest of us, it's pretty hard to live with a heightened sense of awareness all the time, and I'm not sure we would want to. Imagine going through every minute with your heart racing and your emotions set to "high," so that disappointments and sorrows, as well as thrills and joy, would exhaust you with their intensity.

I have a friend who likes to joke that certain dramatic or emotional people tend to run around with their "hair on fire," meaning that they approach life as a constant crisis and emergency. That's not the way to live.

But what if we all ran around with our hearts on fire? Now that's altogether different. It's no coincidence that when the

Holy Spirit came to rest over the believers' heads during Pentecost, it appeared as tongues or flames of fire. We're meant to be set ablaze, to live with a heated passion for God, with our eyes wide open, like the saints and poets, so we can recognize the glory that's often hidden in the plain and ordinary.

We can't all be artists, but we can all learn to see through artists' eyes, becoming awake and aware. Appreciating. Acknowledging. Giving thanks to the Giver of all gifts, great and small.

It's about simplicity, Tom the photographer might say. You've got to be able to take the distracting stuff out of the picture, so you can focus on the good. So you can see the beauty that's hiding in plain sight, just like the little purple flower under the brown pine needles. I expect that Pat might add, don't rush either. We photographers didn't come to the Smokies to just snap an image and rush on to the next place. We could buy a postcard if we were interested in only the scenery. We had come to look and enjoy, yes, but also to learn and grow in knowledge. Aren't we here in life to learn and grow too? Even if we have to slow down and simplify?

Our group of nature photographers had a few days together, and we spent the rest of our time climbing the trails and exploring the rocky streams and old cabins left standing in the incredibly beautiful Tennessee mountains. Once we took an hour to circle around and around a patch of great white trilliums, native wildflowers, waiting until a splash of sunlight illuminated them through a cloud cover to get a perfect shot. At a rest stop we chased a bunch of lemon-yellow butterflies flitting from branch to bloom on a redbud tree, and late one afternoon we walked down to a churning stream where we followed Tom's lead and stretched out on the ground, spread-eagle on top of some really uncomfortable rocks, just to get close-ups of jellylike egg cases that contained tiny tadpoles wiggling and waiting to emerge. Everywhere visitors to the park were on the prowl for woodpeckers and mushrooms, otters and salamanders, wildflowers and black bears.

At last Tom led us to a small waterfall on Pigeon River that splashed over rocks carpeted with thick, emerald-green moss. Beautiful waterfalls are abundant in the Smokies, and Tom, who had been reading a book on theoretical physics, explained that he liked to photograph the flowing water and experiment with the concept of time.

He showed us how to slow the shutter speed and exposure times on our cameras, to capture a soft "bridal veil" effect in the cascade. These small changes made the waterfall appear to freeze in place, so the water looked milky in our finished images. Freezing the passage of time was just a trick, of course, a special effect to use in a photo album.

Real time passes. Life rushes on. As Pat said, the world changes while we're standing in the middle of it, oblivious. We just don't notice until we get up one morning and spot a new wrinkle in the mirror or find a wedding invitation in the mail from a little kid who used to live next door.

The passage of time can feel scary, unless you know the One who is timeless and never-changing, the eternal God who offers us the chance to live forever with him. He is the Maker of the salamanders and toads, of the lichen and the moss, of the sunlight that warms the hills and wakes the birds. He makes each day and puts the goodness in it.

Listen to the Scriptures: "Every generous act and every perfect gift is from above, coming down from the Father of lights" (James 1:17). Each day is a snapshot of grace, when you think about it. Each day is God's gift to us, wrapped in a package that holds twenty-four hours, tied neatly with ribbons of love.

8

A Taste of Honey

Eat honey, my son, for it is good,
and the honeycomb is sweet to your palate;
realize that wisdom is the same for you.
If you find it, you will have a future,
and your hope will never fade.

—Proverbs 24:13–14

*I*t's a little tricky for some of us to understand why beekeepers are so crazy about their hobby. Bees don't usually
come to mind when we're looking for companions to share
our lives, and they certainly don't deliver the warm fuzzies we get
from animals like golden retrievers and Siamese kittens. Most of us
just wave them off as a bunch of flying pests that have an annoying
habit of hovering around our picnic tables and a painful tendency
to sting if we annoy them back.

Then you meet an apiculturist—a beekeeper—like Tony
Casteel, and you start to get a glimpse into his fascination with
this hobby. Tony can become downright poetic as he talks about

keeping honeybees, an interest he inherited from his grand-father, and even though he's a busy electrical contractor whose cell phone chirps all day long, he graciously slips away from his work one afternoon to show me a dozen hives he manages behind his Georgia home.

"There's a fair amount of work involved in beekeeping," Tony admits as he lights a smoker, a beekeeper's tool that looks like a handheld burner with bellows. When he opens one of the large wooden boxes that house his bees, he gently blows a puff of cool smoke into the air, to help calm and control the busy insects while we peer inside.

In part, Tony keeps his bees for their delicious honey, which he collects and processes for his family's use or to give as holiday gifts to his business customers. The Southeast, he says, is one of the country's best honey-producing regions, with a variety of plants that bloom throughout the year. That allows for multiple "honey flows," or periods when the bees can find lots of different kinds of nectar that they'll turn into thick, sweet syrup flavored with the taste of maple, blackberry, orange blossoms, wild-flowers, sourwood, or even cotton.

But Tony, who's on track to earn a master's certificate from a state-certified beekeeping institute, is into this for more than just the honey. "When I see the afternoon sun setting, and the bees flying in and out by the hundreds, I know I'm seeing a healthy hive in action, and it gives me joy," he says. "Beekeeping is a husbandry art, like keeping chickens, goats, or any other sort of herd animal. It's not the individual that you look out for. It's more like caring for a group." He pauses for a moment. "I'm very attached to my bees."

He's not alone. Thousands of ordinary folks are dedicated to keeping hives filled with the hairy little creatures, both for the fascination of observing their complex social systems and for the sweet payoff of the delicious food they produce.

But it's more than just having your own honey makers on hand. For keepers like Tony, being outdoors and working with the hives offer a chance to escape into another world, whether he's cleaning a honeycomb, removing wax, checking periodically for problems stemming from disease or parasites, or simply providing a few basics like clean water and extra food. "I don't care how frustrating my day was; when I'm in the hives, I can totally relax." He grins. "Having thousands of bees crawl on you might not sound relaxing to most people, but it really does help you forget about your troubles."

I'm trying to remember this as Tony helps me suit up in a veiled beekeeper's helmet and roomy overshirt. He's mentioned that one strong colony can hold between fifty and sixty thousand bees, all with stingers firmly attached, so I'm counting on the protective gear to provide that laid-back mood he's talking about.

Although Tony handles his bees skillfully, and they've grown accustomed to having him around, he predicts that he'll get stung at least once while the hive is uncovered, and he does. He doesn't mind so much; he's sold on the idea that bee venom works as a holistic medicine for his arthritic thumb joint. "There's no conclusive evidence for this," he says, "but every time I get stung on the hand, after the pain of the sting fades, my arthritis is gone for about a week."

Despite a few stings now and then, beekeepers agree that their hobby is soothing and habit forming. "It does sound odd," says Robert N. Brewer Jr., a fellow enthusiast, "but beekeeping is the most addictive thing I've ever done. Honeybees are inherently gentle creatures, and they're extremely important to the world's ecosystem."

As a Georgia Agricultural Extension coordinator, Brewer occasionally gets calls from homeowners who want to remove honeybees from their property. "We actually need to encourage [honeybees] as much as possible," he says. "They do 85 to 90 percent of all the food pollination in the country. For a while you didn't see any wild honeybees at all. Fifteen years ago literally millions of colonies were wiped out by a parasite known as the Varroa mite. Now things are starting to improve, and there are wild bees living in hollow trees again."

Anyway, Brewer says, honeybees sting only to defend their homes, or when we're plundering their food stores. "Bees eat honey, too, so it's like we're stealing their groceries," he says with a chuckle.

We've been raiding bee larders for a long time. Archaeologists point to cave drawings in Spain and Africa, some dating back to 700 BC, that depict honey gatherers climbing trees as angry insects swarm around. Ancient Egyptians, who dubbed the honeybee Apis, in honor of one of their gods, had beekeeping down to a fine art, Brewer says. "They took clay jars filled with bees up and down the Nile, to catch the nectar flow of various plants as they came into bloom." They used the honey to flavor cakes, biscuits, and other dishes. In ancient Rome, honey was the primary sweetener for the table, and some historians think it may even have been used as a substitute for gold when paying taxes.

Today beekeepers move their hives from one end of the country to the other on tractor trailers, hiring out their services to farmers whose fields need extra pollination. The portable hives are often in demand because the Varroa mites, which can decimate entire colonies in just days, have created a bee shortage. In recent years almond growers in California, where 80 percent of the nation's almond crop is produced, have had to truck in hives from as far away as Australia to pollinate their trees.[13]

Since bees are so important to our food supply, and because they've been vital to life since ancient times, it's not surprising that the Bible has a lot to say about them.

Samson, who once killed a lion with his bare hands, returned to its carcass to find it swarmed by bees making honey (although bees wouldn't typically mass around a dead animal, scholars think that the desert heat may have desiccated the lion's body and provided a nesting site for them). Samson ate the honey, we're told, and spun from this incident a riddle to taunt the Philistines, but there may be a deeper, hidden meaning in this story. After all, Satan walks about as a lion, too, seeking to devour us with his lies and temptations, but when he's defeated, we can feast on the honey-sweet victory that comes through Jesus.

Unfortunately for the bees, the Scriptures also frequently mention their less desirable traits, like their tendency to sting and chase us around the yard. David, for example, compared his enemies to an angry horde: "All the nations surrounded me . . . They surrounded me like bees; they were extinguished like a fire among thorns; in the name of the LORD I destroyed them" (Ps. 118:10, 12).

Death has a "sting," according to 1 Corinthians, which comes from sin. Yet despite these kinds of comments, I don't think the Scripture writers were really down on bees; it's just that the little insects lend themselves to some useful and memorable metaphors.

It's when you start looking for biblical references to honey, rather than the bees that make it, that you find the praise verses. Honey was so precious, that when God wanted to tell the Israelites about the glorious land he was going to give them, he described it as a place flowing with milk and honey, "the most beautiful of all lands" (Ezek. 20:6). During their forty-year ordeal in desert places, God fed his people with manna that rained down from heaven, a wafer-like food that tasted like coriander seed ground and blended with honey.

When God chose Ezekiel to serve as his prophet, he sent to

him beelike creatures with human forms and wings that roared like rushing water when they flew. The strange beings told Ezekiel to literally ingest a scroll covered on the front and back with words of mourning and grief. "Son of man," one of these creatures commanded, "eat what you find here. Eat this scroll, then go and speak to the house of Israel. So I [Ezekiel] opened my mouth, and He fed me the scroll . . . and it was as sweet as honey in my mouth" (Ezek. 3:1–3).

True sweetness, we discover, is not the honey scraped from a waxy comb, but the Word of God, and in the New Testament we learn that the Word was made flesh in Jesus.

God's Word is "more desirable than gold . . . and sweeter than honey—than honey dripping from the comb," the psalmist declared (Ps. 19:10). When we incorporate God's commandments into our lives, we're satisfied and nourished. The Word is spiritual food for our souls.

Tasting the sweetness of God's Word is as easy as opening your Bible and reading it every day for its holy teachings. "Eat honey, my son, for it is good, and the honeycomb is sweet to your palate; realize that wisdom is the same for you. If you find it, you will have a future, and your hope will never fade" (Prov. 24:13–14).

Once we've fed ourselves on the Word, we can speak it, too, to edify—that is, to encourage and strengthen—ourselves and others. David, whose psalms were often filled with cries for deliverance from his enemies or with expressions of his deep yearning for God, came to realize that God's instructions poured light on the difficult path he had to walk. "How sweet Your word is to my taste—sweeter than honey to my mouth. I gain understanding from Your precepts (Ps. 119:103–4)."

Many everyday foods represent the Word in the Bible. In the book of Hebrews, God's teachings are compared to milk for new followers, infants who are "inexperienced with the message about righteousness" (Heb. 5:13), and who wouldn't be able to digest the more complex message, or solid food, given to mature believers. Later, when they "grow up" in righteousness and can digest adult teachings, they can be given more nourishing and substantial "food" to chew on.

God's Word also tastes as sweet as honey on our lips. Think of this: It's so like God to give us more than what is basic and necessary, so like him to be extravagant in his goodness, grace, and love.

Have you ever looked at a caterpillar's cocoon? Some caterpillars, like those of the monarch butterfly, look like strange, green aliens, with big "eye spots" of color to deter predators who might eat them. Other cocoons are small cigar-shaped cases that look as if they're spun from soft, white threads. Some resemble dry, brown leaves, while others blend right in with green foliage on the trees. They're such little, seemingly insignificant bits of nature—cocoons—and yet I believe that the Creator gave us the wonder and diversity of their colors, shapes, and sizes simply to share the joy and pleasure he felt in making them.

Why should his Word be any different? The Scriptures could have been merely a set of instructions, first given orally, then written down, to command, guide, and lead us, and they do accomplish all those things. But God's Word as transcribed in the Bible is sweet too. Its prose and poetry are delicious for our ears to hear and our hearts to trust, and the pleasure we find in it is just one more unexpected, unmerited gift from a Father who cares so much that he wants not only to communicate but to delight and inspire.

Before I left Tony, my beekeeping friend, he pressed a jar of his homemade wildflower honey into my hands, and it was all I could do to resist dipping my finger into it on the way home. But I waited and shared it with my husband the next morning over breakfast. We dipped spoons into the thick, gold syrup and swirled it over toast. The honey was so rich and sweet, and I marveled at how thousands of tiny bees had turned the nectar collected from hundreds of flowers into something so nutritious and satisfying to eat.

The honey, like the Word, was food for us to savor, and we reveled in its goodness.

Forgiven

*And be kind and compassionate to one
another, forgiving one another,
just as God also forgave you in Christ.*

—Ephesians 4:32

imes were hard in the Depression years. The boy's father worked for the Central of Georgia Railway as a foreman, directing a crew of laborers who laid track all day, every day. Throughout the sweltering summertime when the sun heated up, they hammered down the heavy ties with iron spikes as they smelled the stink of hot creosote and tar. It was brutal work in the Southern humidity and heat, but it was the way the boy's father earned a living, since he had only a third-grade education. In time, the hard work made the man hard too.

The boy's mother helped earn money for the family when she could. She took in washing for a couple of town ladies whose husbands were still able to buy them a nice dress now and then, and she churned butter from the family cow's milk. When she had enough to spare, she sold eggs that she collected each morning from underneath the warm bellies of her little hens.

The family lived in a railroad house, which is to say, a cheap rental shack provided by the company that employed the father. Its high ceilings made it cool in the summertime, but cold air whistled through the wooden walls in the winter, and the heat from the coal stove did little to beat it back. Some days the mother had to break the crust of ice that formed in the toilet bowl, but at least it was an indoor toilet.

The boy was embarrassed to live in the railroad house, because it sat alongside the tracks, and when the train rumbled past every morning, bleary-eyed passengers rocking along inside the cars seemed to look straight through the family's bare windows. The boy lived in a small town where the biggest entertainment was swimming in the local creek, and where sometimes the kids could go see a new Gene Autry movie, if they collected enough glass bottles to turn in for change. But the boy knew enough of the world to know what abundance was and what it wasn't. He lived in want, and he knew it and felt ashamed.

One steamy August afternoon the boy went inside to sit at the kitchen table and watch as his mother made a cake from flour and eggs and a scant cup of sugar. It was going to be a treat, since they didn't often have a lot to eat. Breakfast, lunch, and supper were often "hoecakes" made from cornmeal, salt, and flour, sweetened by a dollop of sorghum syrup. It wasn't healthy food for a growing boy, but it was what many poor families ate.

On this August day, after she had sifted the flour for her cake, the boy's mother stopped and looked at him. He needed a haircut, and for once, she had a little extra money from selling eggs. She lifted down an empty pickle jar from a shelf above the stove and fished out a few coins with her floury fingers. "Take these," she said, "and run to old Jenkins's shop and get you a real haircut.

"For special," she added with a smile, "remind him to give you a peppermint stick from his jar when you're done."

The boy stuck the money in his pocket and tore out through the screen door, letting it slam behind him, already hearing the peppermint stick calling his name. He ran to town, which wasn't far, slapping his jeans just to hear the coins jingle.

When he got there, he peered into the shadowy interior of the little barber shop. Old man Jenkins was tucking a white cloth around somebody's neck, and when he was done, he turned around to the counter to mix shaving soap in a little cup. The boy heard the brush thunk against the sides of the china cup as Jenkins added a few drops of water and stirred until the stuff inside turned to foam.

"Come on in here," Jenkins said when he saw the boy. "Sit yourself down and I'll be with you in a few minutes." Old Jenkins nodded toward another man who was already sitting and waiting. "It'll be his turn next, and then your'n," said the barber.

The boy found a seat in a row of chairs and slid back until he could swing his feet back and forth over the floor. There was a funny smell he hadn't smelled before in Jenkins's shop, and he wrinkled his nose as he glanced over at the other man sitting beside him, the one awaiting his turn for a cut and a shave.

The strange smell was coming from the man. He looked funny too. His eyes seemed heavy, like he was about to go to sleep, and he had his arms crossed over his chest. Sometimes his head nodded down and then he snapped back awake. The boy watched him for a while, and that was a mistake.

When the man noticed that the boy was watching, he shook his head, rubbed his eyes, and stared back. "What are you looking at?" he growled.

The boy didn't answer. He just grabbed up one of the newspapers stacked in a pile on a nearby table. He never talked much at all, and he sure didn't know what to say to a stranger.

"Who is this kid?" the man asked, jerking his thumb toward the boy.

Jenkins didn't look up. "That's Baxter's boy," he said. "Lives around here, but he don't come in much. Do you, boy?"

The boy shook his head. His mama usually trimmed his hair. But this time was special. He saw the jar with the peppermint sticks sitting on the counter behind Jenkins's cash register.

"Baxter?" the man said. He repeated the family's last name, and then he sat there for a minute, blinking in the dimly lit shop.

Finally he turned back around, scowling, to speak to the boy. "That your daddy, the one that's the foreman for the railroad?"

The boy nodded. "Yessir," he said. He shrank back into his chair, suddenly afraid of this stranger.

The man cursed. "I know your daddy," he said, slurring his words. "Cost me my job, threw me off his crew. He's the meanest—" He kept talking, and the boy's ears burned to hear the words.

The boy was crumpling the newspaper in his fingers now, and it was shaking a little from his fear. He didn't know what to say. His face felt very hot, and he looked toward the door, longing to run away.

The man leaned closer and said other things. His breath had a bad smell about it, one the boy didn't recognize until he saw a half-empty bottle sticking out of the man's jacket pocket. Now he knew what was wrong, and yet he had to breathe in the smell, because the man was in his face, and he felt as if he was breathing in the man's anger too. His stomach churned with fear.

The man got louder and more agitated. Finally he told the boy that he should curse his father too. "Go on," the man said. "Call him what he is. Say it!" He was red-faced now.

The boy began to tremble. His father was a stern man, and the boy was not allowed to say bad words. He knew that he'd be punished, and his punishment would be terrible.

The man kept talking until he was almost sputtering. He insisted that the boy call his father, his own father, an ugly, profane name.

"Say it," the man said. He reached out and gave the boy a push on his shoulder.

"Leave him alone, Madison," said Jenkins suddenly. He had stopped lathering and shaving the man in the barber's chair and stood staring at what was happening, his soapy brush suspended in the air. The man with the white towel around his neck stared, too, as if he couldn't believe his eyes, and the veins in his neck bulged and stood out like ropes.

The man called Madison did not stop. He strode over to Jenkins's counter and grabbed up a pair of his sharp scissors.

Jenkins objected, but neither he nor his customer moved.

Madison snarled at him to mind his own business. He walked over to the boy again, staggering a little, and this time he poked him in the shoulder with the tip of the scissors.

The boy was shaking so hard he dropped the newspaper. "Don't," he begged.

The man laughed. "You're not a big man now, are you?" he mocked. He seemed to have forgotten he was talking to the boy, and not his enemy.

He poked the boy again, and this time, the boy saw a tiny slit open in the cloth of his shirt. The boy was crying now, but not letting any sound come out. "Say it!" the man demanded, looming over him. "Say it! Say it!"

At last the boy said the ugly name.

The barber said something, too, and the man getting a shave yanked off his white towel, threw it on the floor, and stood up.

They all stood like statues, and then, finally, the angry man just stopped. He dropped the scissors with a clatter to the floor and sat down heavily in a chair, as if he'd just awoken from a dream. He rubbed his eyes with his fingers and suddenly looked very tired and worn.

The boy, seeing his chance, jumped up and ran out the door, letting the screen slam behind him. Fear made his ears ring, and he didn't answer or stop when he heard Jenkins call his name.

That night, when his father came home, he told the boy to come to him. His father knew what had happened in the barber shop, but he had it wrong. Somebody had told somebody else, and the story had gotten twisted into a lie.

Nothing had been said about the torment from the angry man. All the boy's father knew was that his son had said a profane word. The gossip made it sound like the boy was to blame.

The boy tried to explain, his words rushing and tumbling over one another in his haste and anxiety. But he was just a boy, and his father had heard the tale from another adult, and because he believed the grown-up, he punished the boy. The punishment was harsh, because these were harsh times, and a deep, ugly wound opened up in the boy's heart that day, one that would take a lifetime to heal.

"If only," the boy said many years later, "if only he had had faith in me, how different life would have been. If only he had trusted me."

Ultimately faith is about trust. Faith means knowing another person so well, you are sure of how he acts and what he says, even when you aren't there to witness his deeds and words. Your faith is a kind of deep and intimate knowing.

When we say we believe in God, we are claiming we have that kind of faith, and it finds expression in a close, personal relationship with his Son, Jesus. We're saying that despite the circumstances around us—despite the sin and evil we see in the world—we have confidence that we serve a living Savior who will set things right one day. We know this, because we know him.

Sadly the boy in that barber shop in the little Southern town so many years ago was not believed. I know because that boy was my father, and this story, except for the names of those involved, is true. Some sixty-five years later, shortly before he died, my dad recounted the events of that day to me again. He had recited it to me many times before. Eventually the truth came out, and his father, who was my grandfather, begged for his forgiveness and received it. But the wound from that incident left a scar that never wholly healed, and it changed who my father was.

I've never forgotten the story because, through it, I came to understand more about the meaning of faith.

The incident also taught me that mercy is a gift, that it's about clemency and compassion. It's about showing kindness and gentleness even when, or especially when, those two good gifts are neither deserved nor merited. If you look up the word in a dictionary, you'll find that *mercy* comes from the Medieval Latin *merces*, which means "price paid" or "wages." Mercy is what we plead for from a judge when we stand before him, convicted and guilty, and it is what we need and what we receive from Jesus when we confess our faults and flaws.

The Scriptures tell the story of another son from a long-ago time, a prodigal who came back home after he squandered his inheritance, leaving him desperate. A terrible famine had descended on the land, and the only work he was able to find was on a farm, where he fed another man's pigs. Thin and weak, he may have even resorted to stealing carob pods from the swines' trough, just to fill his rumbling belly.

But because he had a glimmer, a tiny spark of desperate hope left in his heart, one day he left the pigs behind and stumbled home to his father. *Maybe*, he thought, *if I can just make it down one more road, survive one more weary day, I can throw myself at my father's feet and plead for scraps to eat.* The boy may have been afraid that his stern and disappointed father would tell him to get out of his sight, that he would shout that he had been given too much already, only to waste it all, and that now he would have to fend for himself back in the pigsty.

Then something incredible happened. As the prodigal son approached his former home, his father came out. The father didn't walk toward him, his face contorted by anger, shaking his fist in the air, but ran—ran!—to meet him, maybe even crushing him in a bear hug that nearly cracked the boy's ribs, weeping with joy, laughing, and calling to everyone else to come outside. "Quick! See who has come home." The father lavished kisses on his son's cheeks and then ordered the servants to bring clean clothes and sandals and to prepare plenty of good food. "You were dead to us," the father said, tears pouring down his face, "but you're back. You're home, alive and safe."

What a profound difference mercy makes, and how it heals and restores.

We are all, in the end, that wayward, lost son who deserves the punishment, and yet if we confess our sins, he is faithful and just to forgive.

But there's another aspect to forgiveness. Life isn't just about being absolved of your own wrongdoing and sin; it's also about granting forgiveness to those who wrong you. Corrie ten Boom, a Dutch Christian who helped the Jews during World War II and later survived imprisonment in a Nazi concentration camp, held on to Jesus in spite of losing most of her beloved family and enduring terrible suffering. Although she struggled, she managed to obey Jesus, who told Peter to forgive someone who harmed him not seven times, but "70 times seven" (Matt. 18:22). She wrote in her book, *Tramp for the Lord*, that the ability to forgive come through the power of the Holy Spirit.[14]

God's forgiveness is a gift, and it's also a gift to forgive others.

There are so many small things, little mercies that we have to train our eyes to see and our ears to catch, but the ultimate grace we can receive is forgiveness and reconciliation through Jesus.

Next to that, I think, is the forgiveness we show one another. When it comes to that kind of mercy—well, forgiveness may be the biggest and best gift of all.

Hang Gliding

If I go up to heaven, You are there.

—Psalm 139:8

or someone who likes to swim and snorkel in the ocean, I thought it wouldn't be terribly hard to learn to hang glide. Instead of balancing on a boat platform bobbing up and down over the waves, waiting for the right moment to step off into the sea, I'd only have to take a few running steps off a bunny slope to launch myself into a deep blue "ocean" of air.

Well, OK. Maybe novice hang gliders don't exactly soar thousands of feet above the earth in an ocean of air. They actually learn this sport by flying a short distance over a nice, relatively safe, and flat stretch of ground. In spite of a bit of vertigo when I'm in high places, I thought hang gliding could be a real rush. It appealed to my sense of adventure and my overly romantic imagination, in which I saw myself sailing serenely along under the butterfly-bright wings of a glider. If flying took my breath away, I figured I'd just catch it back after an initial rush of excitement and then settle down to ride the wind.

I imagined all this stuff because for years, we'd taken weekend trips into the nearby mountains where we often passed a popular hang gliding school. On fair-weather days, the hang gliders seemed to float over the valley below—soaring, dipping, and rising until they were ready to land gracefully in a wide green field where one of the school's four-wheelers waited to ferry both flyer and glider back up the mountain.

I was tempted to try it myself. It looked like so much fun, such a thrill.

One October I decided to explore the possibility of learning to fly. Fall was an excellent time, Matt, the manager of the flying park, told me. Daytime highs in the mountains averaged around sixty degrees, so the temperature and visibility were usually good. As a beginner, Matt explained, I'd go up in a tandem glider, a craft built to accommodate a student and an experienced instructor. An ultralight plane would tow us to about two thousand feet above the valley floor—so no solo jumps off the bunny slope, after all—and once we crossed over the Tennessee River below us, we could expect to glimpse the city of Chattanooga, Tennessee, in the distance, some forty minutes away by car.

As a beginner, Matt said, my job was simply to lie prone in

a harness connected to the airframe, poised like Superman with my hands held out in front of me, and let my instructor do the actual flying. Experienced gliders could soar for three hours or more, reaching elevations of six thousand feet or more.

Matt became more and more enthusiastic as he described the adventure ahead of me. Occasionally hang gliders got a real bird's-eye view, he said—of real birds. Flyers had reported looking at the wing tips and finding hawks, buzzards, and even eagles soaring alongside. "Sometimes an eagle will come by and whap the top of a sail," he said, "but they just bounce off."

Eagles. And "whapping." I felt a stir of anxiety. Having a creature with razor-sharp talons hit your sail sounded like a pretty big problem to me. "Wouldn't the birds rip the wing with their talons?" I asked. "Or worse, attack the people flying the glider?"

"I think they're trying to say, 'Move out of my territory,'" Matt said—which reassured me but didn't exactly answer the question—"and when it doesn't work, they go away."

Anyway, Matt insisted, the thrill was worth it. Hang gliding could feel like a roller-coaster ride, except that I'd feel myself moving freely in three dimensions instead of simply forward on a track. I hated to tell someone who clearly loved his sport, but I wasn't a huge fan of roller-coaster rides; in fact, they hurt my back and made my stomach flip. I trusted him, I really did, and I knew the gliding school enjoyed a great safety record and an equally great reputation. But the romance of the idea was beginning to fade as reality set in. I might actually have to get out there and do this! With predatory birds that jealously guarded their airspace, and unpredictable wind currents that could lift you one moment and send you plunging earthward in the next.

Matt must have sensed the chicken coming out in me, especially when I asked about holding on to the control bar in the glider for security, something I particularly liked to do on sky lifts, as if clinging to the center rod in the bucket would really help if the whole thing went crashing to the ground. No, Matt said gently, it would not be necessary or desirable for me to grip the bar tightly. I should place my hands on it lightly because a slight touch would shift our direction, and besides, the instructor would handle that part.

There wouldn't be much noise while I was gliding, Matt added, unless I heard an occasional bark from a dog in the valley below or a little whistle that wind often made when it came off the glider's wings. Surfing on invisible waves of air, he assured me, was a spiritual experience.

Hang gliding was going to be a spiritual experience for me, too, I realized, since I was going to need a lot of faith to carry out my plan to try it. I had confidence in the instructors, to be sure. Hundreds of students had learned to fly with them—and land—safely, but suddenly my courage was ready to take a hike. Eagles might not sink their claws into me, but fear sure did.

The flight school instructors were very understanding. After all, fear is an emotion that crosses all boundaries, including time, if you think about it. Today, we're scared and worried about so many things, like getting a job, failing a class, finding a lump, losing a pension, living alone, missing a payment, or raising a family.

People in biblical times weren't so different. In the Old Testament stories, men worried about going into battle, finding good land for their crops and water for their sheep and cattle, and providing an inheritance for their children. Sarai, before she became Sarah, feared that she could never be able to give her husband, Abram, a baby, until God changed Abram's name to Abraham and promised he'd become the father of nations.

Moses was afraid he couldn't speak eloquently enough to persuade Pharaoh to let God's people leave Egypt, and then he worried about how to lead them if he did. God knew Moses was capable, but to answer his fears, he sent Moses' brother, Aaron, to help him and filled both their mouths with the words they needed to say.

"Why are you fearful?" Jesus once asked his disciples, when their boat was caught in a violent storm on the lake (Mark 4:40). The Master had been teaching on the hillside that day, telling a crowd about the kingdom of God, and earlier, when the people became hungry and restless, he'd performed a miracle with loaves and a few fish to feed them all. You'd think his disciples would have learned. But when the sun set, the men decided to move their boat to the other shore, and soon they were frightened again.

Under the darkening sky, the wind began to rise, slamming waves against the boat and filling it with water, but incredibly Jesus almost slept through the whole thing. His disciples had to go to the stern, where he lay on a cushion, and wake him, saying in voices that must have been stricken with terror, "Teacher! Don't you care that we're going to die?" (Mark 4:38). It took only a word from Jesus for the storm to be stilled. "Why are you fearful?" he asked the shaken men. "Do you still have no faith?" (Mark 4:40).

In the book of Matthew, Jesus also reassured his anxious disciples not to fret about food or clothes, because their heavenly Father would provide those material things. And what about Mary, when she ran to Jesus anguished and weeping because he arrived too late to save her ailing brother Lazarus? Jesus may have delayed his visit to demonstrate his power over everything, including death, and at his command Lazarus rose from the dead, putting Mary's grief in the grave instead. The list goes on and on; every fear is answered with reassurance and perfect love.

To his credit, Paul, who never even met the living Lord, figured this out. He listed in 2 Corinthians the floggings, beatings, and imprisonment he suffered for Christ's sake. Three times he was shipwrecked as he traveled to share the gospel, and once he was lost at sea. He crossed dangerous rivers, encountered robbers and false "friends," and endured sleepless nights, hunger, thirst, and cold. "There is the daily pressure on me," he wrote (2 Cor. 11:28), and he prayed often that God would remove an unspecified "thorn in the flesh" (2 Cor. 12:7) that caused him grief. As far as we know, Paul had to deal with that thorn throughout the rest of his life, yet he still praised God. His secret? He clung to Jesus, who promised, "My grace is sufficient for you, for power is perfected in weakness" (2 Cor. 12:9). When fear raised its ugly head, Paul beat it back with faith.

I love what my friend Mary once wrote to me, about how we have our big human emotions and our big God, who can take a "too-big thing and make it small and manageable for us. The greatest fear we can have is overcome by the greatness of our God and His way, which is complete peace, stillness, comfort, security, and confidence."

Mercy, Mary went on to say, translates to kindness, which translates to favor, and "God has uncountable ways of blessing His children with His mercy. His blessings may appear to be very small from our perspective, yet His mercy is tremendous, as He is. He is so powerful, so big, so mighty, and so great." Amen!

The opposite of faith, I've heard it said, isn't doubt. It's fear. Fear is one of my ongoing "thorns in the flesh," because even though I believe in God, I do wrestle with worry and anxiety sometimes.

Not that fear is always a bad thing. At least that's what I told myself as I stood there twisting my hair nervously, mulling over the idea of soaring through the air strapped into a tandem glider. As I said, I've still got a few tiny problems to work out.

I might or might not leap into the sky in the glider, but I decided I could fling my fears away, at least. I closed my eyes and remembered, "The one who lives under the protection of the Most High dwells in the shadow of the Almighty . . . you will take refuge under His wings" (Ps. 91:1, 4).

Standing on the edge of the mountain, a steady breeze blowing through my hair, I understood what Matt meant about the exhilaration and excitement of hang gliding. Everyone who has tried it enthuses that there's such a freedom in flying, even if that first launch into the blue sky requires a leap of faith. You just have to believe that what you're doing is worth the risk, because there's so much to gain.

There's a freedom when your spirit soars, too, when you throw yourself into God's care and entrust him with every moment of your life, sure that his mercy imposes no conditions and has no limits. You jump and discover that he'll catch and hold you fast. "The heavens are Yours; the earth also is Yours" (Ps. 89:11).

"Do you not know? Have you not heard? Yahweh is the everlasting God, the Creator of the whole earth. He never grows faint or weary; there is no limit to His understanding. He gives strength to the weary and strengthens the powerless. Youths may faint and grow weary, and young men stumble and fall, but those who trust in the LORD will renew their strength; they will soar on wings like eagles; they will run and not grow weary; they will walk and not faint" (Isa. 40:28–31).

Bob and the Beast

*How little people know who think that
holiness is dull . . . When one meets
the real thing, it's irresistible.*

—C. S. Lewis

T he firemen were coming on the Monday after Easter
weekend. That explained why I found myself hunched
over the kitchen table with my son, Michael, one Sunday
afternoon, both of us trying to wrestle a raw egg into a nest of
Bubble Wrap and tape. Michael, nine years old at the time, was
still willing to let his mom help him, although he was becoming
fiercely independent too. Despite my protests, he was insistent on
adding the morning newspaper, which I hadn't had time to read
yet, around his egg, named Bob, for extra protection.

And protection was the name of this game. School had recessed
for spring break, during which Easter fell, and Easter is, after all,

a very egg-friendly holiday. Each kid in my son's fourth-grade class had been assigned a task. Every child was to devise his or her own way to pad an egg so it wouldn't shatter when dropped from a height of thirty feet.

For more excitement—and what egg-based activity doesn't beg for some bling—a local fireman had agreed to come and help with the egg fling when the kids returned to class on Monday morning. The entire elementary school would turn out to see him climb onto the roof and drop one egg after another to the sidewalk below. To win the contest and receive a small prize, a student had to wrap his egg so that it would survive the fall.

The kids were actually supposed to be doing a science project on velocity, but as a writer, I couldn't resist looking for a life lesson in their experiment. To me, the exercise felt a lot like an average day in the life of an average person. Most of us are just regular folks, I figured. We're not celebrities who demand bowls of nothing but blue M&Ms to snack on in our dressing rooms. Crowds of fans don't follow us around asking for advice or autographs. Oprah doesn't call, and the paparazzi wouldn't waste a single flash on our photos. We're the ordinary folks, the ones who throw ourselves out there, into the world, every day, as we work at the office, shop for groceries, help the kids with their homework, and walk the dog.

So how does the world receive us for being such regular guys? Well, not always with open arms. Our fragile egos (*ego* is only one letter of the alphabet away from the word *egg*, if you think about it) can get pretty smashed and broken. Does your manager notice how much you hustle to refill your customer's water glass and serve his table? Is your husband truthful when he says your new jeans look fine from the back? Why don't more people eat the casserole you always bake for your book club's potluck dinner? See what I mean? So often we fling our hard work, hopes, and dreams out there into the unknown, praying our best efforts won't end up shattered.

The world receives Christians much the same way. Being a believer isn't the in thing these days. I don't mean we suffer anything like the persecution that Christians face in some parts of the world, where meeting in prayer or giving away a Bible can lead to imprisonment or even death.

But even in our simple, everyday ways, we are a bit like fragile eggs—the raw ones, something like poor Bob in his newspaper cocoon. Coworkers sometimes avoid us believers in the break room or at the lunch table, because they know we don't want to hear the kinds of jokes they tell. Instead of thanks and understanding, we may hear snickers and glimpse rolled eyes when we offer to pray for someone or invite an unchurched person to worship with us. To much of the world, being a believer isn't cool.

Jesus warned us that things would be this way. He told his followers that brothers would betray brothers, fathers their children, children their parents, and that those who follow him would be hated because of his name. And yet he also taught that to sacrifice or suffer for him is to know we are on the right path. Hang on until the end, and, yes, you'll receive your reward in heaven, but you can also take comfort in the joy and peace that comes from a willing and obedient heart.

I'm looking forward to heaven, but even here and now I know we're not alone. God is our ever-present protection. Listen to these words of reassurance: "Do not fear, for I am with you; do not be afraid, for I am your God. I will strengthen you; I will help you; I will hold on to you with My righteous right hand" (Isa. 41:10).

In egg-speak, if you'll forgive me, no matter how the world tosses us around, we are safe because God has his hand on us. We're secure in the Bubble Wrap, you might say, of God's care.

Wouldn't it be great if everyone could know that God loves us so much, that he gave his only Son as a sacrifice for our sin? He is "lovingly devoted" to us, says the psalmist. He won't let us strike a foot against a stone. His angels have been put in charge of our protection, and when we abide with him, he will satisfy us with eternal salvation.

Jesus said that we have to have a child's heart and an innocent faith to enter the kingdom of God, for without faith, it's impossible to please God.

I love children, and I love playing like a child, so I loved Egg Drop Day at Michael's school, because it was silly and fun and filled with laughter, and because even in such a goofy little contest, I could see the love between the teachers and the children they taught; I felt it even from the friendly fireman who gave up his afternoon to climb up on a school roof and pitch eggs packaged in tape, newspaper, and cotton balls into the air. I saw Jesus when I saw the kids laughing, happy to be outdoors on a sunny spring morning when they could run, play, and make noise with nobody shushing them. "Don't stop the little children from coming to me," Jesus had said, "because they're the ones who will inherit my kingdom."

One by one, our volunteer fireman began heaving the packaged eggs from the school roof, and when he was down to his last dozen, it was finally time for poor old Bob. Michael thought his entry looked good, although I had my doubts. The only other egg to beat, Michael assured me, was a competitor nicknamed the Beast, a name he'd gotten for his giant size, which was remarkable even for the carton of extra-large eggs he'd arrived in.

We all stood around on the ground, watching, heads tilted back and hardly daring to breathe, as the fireman tossed the last few padded, boxed, or otherwise-cushioned eggs from the top of the school. The crowd groaned and moaned as parachutes failed, balloons burst, and beach balls exploded. So far, it was omelets all the way.

Then the Beast made a successful descent, the only egg, so far, not to wind up scrambled on the lawn, and his proud owner snatched him up and did a victory dance worthy of a professional football player in the Super Bowl.

Bob was up next. Plain, ordinary old Bob, nested in nothing more than yesterday's news and a scrap of Bubble Wrap left over from the previous Christmas.

Would he make it? Could he survive the fall?

If Bob comes through this, I thought as I waited, so could all of us, all the regular Joes and Janes who don't have beast-sized bank accounts, golden parachute career packages, and private jets waiting to whisk us off to vacation homes in the tropics. We're just grounded in the ordinary stuff of life, most of us, trying hard to follow Jesus and cultivate the childlike faith he desires. But is that enough to cushion us when we're thrown and tossed around in life?

If Bob survived, I decided, the rest of us could too. We wouldn't end up splattered on the sidewalks of the world, instead of rising to the top like a glorious soufflé, because we know whom we have believed. The world couldn't conquer us, because Jesus had our backs.

The fireman stepped to the edge. He picked Bob up and hefted him in both hands. He looked down at the crowd, and we looked up at him. He lifted his arms and let go.

Bob was launched.

He landed.

We peeled away his packing and found him cracked but

unbroken. No yellow streak of yolk betrayed his ordeal. Bob had made it.

We took it as a sign for believers everywhere. May the good eggs always win.

Yellowstone

This is what the LORD says: Stand by the
roadways and look. Ask about the ancient paths:
Which is the way to what is good? Then take it
and find rest for yourselves.

—Jeremiah 6:16

*T*he expedition needed "good hunters," Meriwether Lewis wrote to fellow explorer William Clark, "stout, healthy, unmarried men, accustomed to the woods and capable of bearing bodily fatigue in a pretty considerable degree."

When I visited Yellowstone National Park a few years ago, the only shooting equipment I had at hand was a camera, and with nothing but dinky bear bells tied to my hiking boots to warn off any grizzlies, I'm sure I wouldn't have made the cut for Lewis and Clark's famous journey of 1804–06 into the unmapped West.

It didn't matter. I didn't visit Yellowstone to conquer any new territories or bag any beaver skins; I was there, in part, for a quick family vacation and to do a little research on an early explorer named John Colter as well. Although that old mountain man spelled his last name differently from ours, according to a legend—our carefully cultivated family legend, to be perfectly honest—Colter was a very distant relative of my husband's. That appealed to Bill, who is a mountain lover anyway, and to me, since I'm a pushover for heroic tales and long-ago stories.

John Colter, one guidebook told me, got his start out West when he shouldered his Hawken rifle and enlisted as a private on Lewis and Clark's trip in the 1800s for the going rate of about $55 a month. Apparently he didn't have the advantage of bells for his boots, because the book went on to say that he had a brush with a grizzly, a fearsome beast known among the explorers as a "white bear." Unable to get off a killing round or find a tall tree to climb, Colter escaped by running deep into the Missouri River, a move I'd rather put down to a streak of good common sense running through our family, than any lack of courage.

I don't know what our distant ancestor may or may not have thought about God, but it's hard to read his story without believing that God had his hand on him, because while the mountain man escaped that angry bear, his troubles were just beginning.

Game was abundant in the region that the Lewis and Clark Expedition traveled, and no doubt Colter had heard that fur trappers were making their fortunes on rivers like the Missouri, which ran dark with beavers back in those days. By 1806 Colter asked to be released from his duty, so he could go into business with traders from Illinois. Captain Clark readily agreed, penning a letter for Colter to carry that stated he was a volunteer who had served the company well, and wishing him great success.

By the next winter, my research showed, Colter found work at a large outpost. Its traders sent Colter and another man to trap secretly in Blackfoot country, where competing with the native peoples for game could get a man killed, and indeed, tribesmen soon found the men's traps and captured them. As punishment for invading their territory, and partly for sport, the Indians took away Colter's clothes—all of them, leaving him bare as the day of his birth—and told him if he could outrun them, to go for it. Weaponless and exposed, John literally ran for his life and somehow managed to survive, trekking through hundreds of miles of wilderness before making his way back to the trading post, alone and limping.

Lost, hungry, frightened, pursued. Isn't this story beginning to sound a bit like the story of David? David, the son of Jesse, started out, like John Colter, as a young volunteer who wanted to help the leader of a great endeavor—in this case, King Saul's battle against the Philistines. But while David succeeded in slaying the Israelites' enemy, Goliath, he wound up on the run, too, when Saul later turned on him, jealous that God favored David more than himself.

David fled, first taking refuge in a cave and then wandering on and on through the wilderness as Saul chased at his heels. Yet "God did not hand David over to him" (1 Sam. 23:14). He had a plan for David to become king over Israel and Judah, and from his lineage, Jesus would be born.

One day David would write about what he had endured and about how God rescued him and led him through wilderness places and lonely days. His meditations and songs became some of the psalms that testify to God's protection and guidance. "You observe my travels and my rest; You are aware of all my ways. . . . Where can I go to escape Your Spirit? Where can I flee from Your presence? If I go up to heaven, You are there; if I make my bed in Sheol, You are there. . . . Your right hand will hold on to me" (Ps. 139:3, 7–8, 10). For all the hardships he endured, the years spent in hiding, the near misses with death, the betrayals, and backsliding, David was still a man after God's own heart, and God kept his hand on his life. We know God favored David because of the Bible stories that some of us have heard since childhood.

John Colter told stories of escape and danger, too—not in written form though. For all we know, Colter may have been illiterate, because none of his writings have survived, if indeed they existed in the first place. And if Colter ever spoke words of praise to the God who saved him—if he believed in God at all—we don't have any record of that either.

If not for John Colter—well, Americans were on the move, and explorers and adventurers would have found Yellowstone's natural wonders eventually. But don't discount the power of recounting what you've seen, heard, and experienced. Surely

Colter never imagined that the dangerous, frightening landscape he traveled would turn out to be one of the country's most popular tourist destinations—yet it did.

When Colter finally found his way home and fell into the arms of his fellow frontiersmen, he started babbling about the places he'd been. There were cracks in the ground and holes and fissures, he insisted, where blasts of steam shot up out of the earth or where mud bubbled and burbled in sulphurous pits. He reported seeing Indians catch a fish in one stream and cook it in another. Colter's former employers, Lewis and Clark, incorporated much of what their old friend saw into a report they compiled for President Thomas Jefferson about their journey. Word also circulated about Colter over kitchen tables and campfires, and his legend probably grew taller with each retelling.

Over the years more stories spread about the discoveries being made out West. New trappers flooded into the area to make their fortune, along with hunters, missionaries, and prospectors lured by news of gold strikes in Montana. Influential businessmen toured the region and pronounced it strangely beautiful—easy to say when you don't have hostile natives nipping at your heels.

The government decided to send geologists to chart this wilderness area and confirm its value, and by 1872 the place where John Colter made the run of his life was set aside for the public enjoyment as Yellowstone, the nation's first national park. Now the wonders Colter had raved about were verified, and today Colter is widely credited with having found Yellowstone's largest lake and many of its boiling springs, stewing mud pots, and spewing geysers. Sadly, he passed away in 1813, long before he could enjoy his fame. I suspect that during his lifetime, when he found himself jumping over those hissing vents and smelling brimstone, he may have thought he'd already departed this earthly life, and that all those years of fighting Indians and dodging bears had finally caught up with him.

Nowadays visitors flock into Yellowstone from all over the world, eager to appreciate its majesty. They come, as I did, for its bounty, its sheer extravagance of hot springs and cold rivers, its sweep of alpine meadows and lodgepole pines.

Parts of Yellowstone look positively primeval, but the park is also filled with more familiar beauties. In autumn elk clash their heavy racks, and each winter bison warm their shaggy coats around the steaming pools. Gray wolves roam freely here once again, after a long and misguided banishment.

You have only to look around Yellowstone to know that a generous Artist colored this place. Everywhere terraces and geysers are frosted with multicolored minerals like icing on a cake. Lemonade Lake sparkles lime-yellow, while the springs at Black Sand Basin run as red and orange as canned tomato soup. An explosion of algae has turned Emerald Pool a brilliant green. Talk about living color! At night the sky is a spill of dark ink pierced by glittering white stars.

Yellowstone is God's handiwork, and in such a landscape

his power is revealed in often violent ways, but it would be a loss to harness its wonders. Its mysteries inspire us; its wilderness refreshes jaded souls and tired spirits. Who would want to tame it and spoil the show? Better that an August sky pelts us with sudden hail or a walk in a grassy field flushes a coyote stalking mice.

In spite of the seasonal crowds, there are plenty of places in Yellowstone where you can go to sit in perfect stillness, the quiet broken only by an elk's occasional bugle or the bellow of steam erupting from a geyser. It's a magnificent place to contemplate the Maker, in a landscape that inspires you to reflect on your own soul-scape.

Any place can serve, of course, if you want to examine your heart and draw closer to God. You don't have to go to a park or even outside your room to consider how our lives, however small and insignificant we may think they are, fit into God's plan. God meets us wherever we are—even if, like David and John Colter, we spend some time wandering in the wilderness. That's what the Lord meant in Jeremiah when he urged us to stand by the road for a while and look around; that is, stand still in our lives and think about who we are and how we're living. Then we're to ask about the ancient way, the old path, the "good way" that leads to God, and take it. That's where we'll find rest.

We can't always see what part we are meant to play in God's story, but we can accept our roles willingly, even enthusiastically, and trust in his provision and guidance. After all, who would have expected a shepherd boy with a slingshot to became a king and lead a nation? Who would have thought that a rough frontiersman would stumble across a place so rare and beautiful, the leader of a young country would decide to preserve it for future generations? God can take the smallest beginning and turn it into a great ending.

The next time you find yourself wandering, maybe feeling lost, confused, and even afraid, remember what God does with wilderness people, and be encouraged. "Trust in the LORD with all your heart, and do not rely on your own understanding; think about Him in all your ways, and He will guide you on the right paths" (Prov. 3:5–6).

13

Making Biscuits

Give us today our daily bread.

—Matthew 6:11

Whack and whomp until your arm is sore, but you'll never convince me that you can find a cardboard can of biscuits, the kind you slam against the counter to open, that can hold a stick of butter to the homemade kind.

It's taste I'm talking about, the good old-fashioned flavor of handmade biscuits, hot from the oven and flakey-soft inside, as opposed to those refrigerated, premade lumps of dough. Down South, we call our biscuits "catheads," not because the family feline has anything to do with them, but because we make each one as big and round as—well, a cat's head, hence the name.

Catheads are simply homemade concoctions of flour, milk, and shortening that can barely be described by the humble term *biscuits.* By definition, they are two-handed baked goods, soft and plump as pillows, tender, feather-light, and fluffy.

Our biscuits just beg to be heaped with dollops of pear preserves or strawberry jam. Broken apart, the cathead steams heartily. Buttered, it melts in your mouth, Even finicky children eat them enthusiastically, stuffing them into their mouths until butter and jelly smear their faces and trickle down onto their pajamas. The family dog deigns to eat them too. (Am I making it clear that we love our homemade catheads?)

It takes a passionate cook to make real biscuits, in these hurried, harried times we live in, like the ones my grandmother used to make. Once I watched as Grandma tried to teach me how to prepare them. "Like this," she said, scooping two fingers full of shortening straight from the can. "Now, work it in."

Recipe books call for a pastry cutter to blend your ingredients, but Grandma used her fingers, pinching the shortening and flour together until her bowl was full of pea-sized crumbs. Then she pushed the mixture to the sides of her dough bowl to form a well and poured in a generous glug of buttermilk. How much buttermilk? "Just till it looks right," she'd say.

She kneaded with the heels of her hands, folding the dough over and working it down. A dusting of flour kept it from sticking, and she worked until the feel of the dough told her it had reached the right consistency and elasticity.

Grandma shaped her biscuits by rolling balls of dough between her palms until they became as smooth and round as river stones. Then she tucked the balls side by side into a cake pan, so they'd rise high instead of spreading wide, and finished up by dribbling a cup of melted butter over their tops. It took them only ten minutes to brown, and when they were ready, we slipped them out of the oven and stood there, tossing hot biscuits from hand to hand, until they were cool enough to eat.

Try as I will, I can't duplicate them. Mine are tough and coarse, fit only for doorstops and not the palate, or so soft and insubstantial, they fall apart into your lap at the first bite.

This saddens me. Grandma's cooking was from the heart, perfected by touch, taste, and sight, and it was an art. Today's shrink-wrapped baked goods are packed with preservatives and sold in supermarkets as big as football stadiums, all in the name of convenience, but I'd argue that home cooking shouldn't be lost just because it isn't quick anymore.

Then again, maybe I should be grateful for the availability of ready-made foods. I don't want to sound like the Israelites, who started complaining about their lack of bread shortly after they fled Egypt in search of the Promised Land. By the time they arrived in a region known as the Wilderness of Sin—a place all of us have visited, although the geography isn't necessarily the same—they were griping to Moses and Aaron that they should've stayed in their slavery, because at least "we sat by pots of meat and ate all the bread we wanted" (Exod. 16:2–3). And now where they were, they grumbled? Starving, all of them!

So God did what God always does. He provided. This time he made a breadlike food rain down from heaven for the hungry mob, and not just a slice or two here and there; not crusts or crumbs, but abundant bread (Exod. 16:12).

Scholars who have done their research say this wasn't the plain, bleached-flour bread we use for toast and sandwiches, but a substance that fell in fine flakes and lay like hoar frost on the earth, until the hot sun popped out each morning to melt it. At night, the flakes fell so thickly that there was enough for each person in a household to gather up to two quarts a day, and more to use on the sixth day of the week, so the people could feast on the Sabbath without having to work.

The Israelites called this food manna, and the Scriptures tell us that it was white and small, resembling coriander seed, yet it tasted like wafers sweetened with honey. Moses instructed the people to set two quarts of manna aside after they had eaten. This manna was not to be used and instead would be a reminder to future generations to remember God's faithfulness while they journeyed to their homeland. The manna was to be a spiritual marker to show how God fed both body and soul, providing food for the stomach, strength for the journey, and hope for the heart.

I've read various theories about what manna could have been made of. Some scholars suggest that it came from a lichen, *Lenora esculenta*,[15] which, when dried, would be carried on the wind and blown into the Israelites' camp each day. When ground up, the lichen could be mixed with additives to bake a kind of bread, but it's known to be low in nutritional value, so historians doubt that it could have really supported people on a strenuous expedition in extreme circumstances. (Besides, who knows what dried lichen would have tasted like, no matter how long you baked it?)

Other writers have explained away manna as a hardened, sugary gum or a honey-sweet juice that seeps out of certain desert-dwelling trees.[16] Since I don't have a problem believing that the Creator can do anything he wants with any part of his creation for any purpose he desires, I have no problem believing that manna was miraculously and divinely provided out of nothing but God's will.

However this miraculous bread was produced, while the Israelites continued to complain throughout the rest of their journey, forgetting again and again how God helped them in hard times, at least some of the travelers remembered the daily manna. The writer of Psalm 78 urged his readers to tell their children and their children's children about God's wonderful works: "He rained manna for them to eat; He gave them grain from heaven. People ate the bread of angels" (vv. 24–25).

The bread of angels. How amazing that the One who made the universe loves us so deeply and completely that he feeds us what the angels eat. The psalmist's mission was accomplished; he reminded his generation of God's abundant blessings. But God continues to impress us with his mercy today.

Several times during Jesus' life, his followers asked him for a sign that God had sent him. Despite the miracles and healings he'd already performed and his many teachings, as he sat by Capernaum to speak to a crowd, some people were looking for more proof of the Messiah's identity.

Jesus knew their hearts. I can imagine he may have felt a wave of sadness when he basically told them that he knew why they were there and that it was not really about seeing him, but experiencing the physical benefits of the miracles he performed. They were there for the material things they thought he could give them, and they believed he'd come to lead an earthly kingdom and pursue power and influence, like a mortal man.

I can imagine Jesus sadly shaking his head and reprimanding them, "Don't work for the food that perishes but for the food that lasts for eternal life, which the Son of Man will give you, because God the Father has set His seal of approval on Him" (John 6:27).

Nobody understood. They pressed him. "Our fathers ate the manna in the wilderness" (v. 31). "Where's *your* sign? We want to see something with our physical eyes. We want something delicious to put in our mouths and stomachs. We want an earthly leader with a crown and a throne!"

Of course these questioners aren't so different from a lot of us are today. No matter what God has done for us in the past, we're constantly forgetting. That's why we suffer anxiety and fear and sleepless nights. I do my share of worrying, too, because it's my old and unwanted habit to look to the future with trepidation, rather than remembering how far I've already come. I should be taking confidence and courage and hope, and crazy, wild joy from my heavenly Father's unfailing guidance.

Jesus answered the crowd that stood before him by saying, "*I* am the bread of life." *He* was the sign they were demanding. "I am the bread of life. Your fathers ate the manna in the wilderness, and they died. This is the bread that comes down from heaven so that anyone may eat of it and not die. I am the living bread that came down from heaven. If anyone eats of this bread he will live forever. The bread that I will give for the life of the world is My flesh" (John 6:48–51).

I wonder if the Israelites who ate the manna in the desert actually passed down stories to their children. Did they sit by their beds as the children went to sleep at night, spinning stories of God's presence in desperate places? Did they pray with them at mealtimes, thanking him for each bite? How will our own kids know, if we don't tell them what we believe, and why?

The pastor at our church reminds us that we're supposed to be disciples. We're not supposed to worry so much about how to get people to come into our church building, but we're supposed to concentrate on how we can go out to meet them, so we can talk about our God and introduce him to them, and become living, breathing witnesses to the Savior's grace and power.

How will anyone know, if they don't hear about the Bread that feeds the soul?

When I bake biscuits at home, from scratch—which, I admit, I seldom do anymore—I think about how baking is becoming a lost art. My creations are either flat pancakes or hard little balls you could pitch to the batter in a baseball game. I've tried to carry on with my grandmother's good cooking, but I can see that I'm flopping, big-time, at preserving on this almost lost art of baking.

"Don't worry," my family likes to say, patting me on the back when my cakes fall apart and my biscuits crumble in their fingers. "Canned biscuits are good enough."

I kept trying, though, because I wanted to be able to learn the skill and pass it on to my son. I didn't want his generation, so well-versed in microchips and wireless communications, to grow up wondering what a dough bowl was, or a rolling pin. From the time he was a little boy, I wanted to let him perch on a stool beside me in the kitchen and make a mess over a bowl of flour and milk, so he could experiment and play and learn, and share the fun and satisfaction of making something out of what seemed like nothing.

I never did become a great baker. But surprisingly my husband did. He practiced over and over alongside us, until he was whipping up tender biscuits, fluffy pancakes, tasty breads, and more. So far, he's proved to be an excellent teacher and role model for our son, who is grown now and doing some cooking for himself in his college dorm.

Nothing can match the warmth of a kitchen heated by a slow oven on a chilly morning, and nothing matches the simple, authentic pleasure a parent feels when he or she slows her pace and spends time teaching a child, even if that child soon grows tall enough to look down at the top of your head. Nothing matches the deep, pure joy of teaching your child about the Bread of Life, either, the Bread of salvation, the food from heaven that lasts forever.

So teach what you know. Don't let the next generation forget. Pass it on.

Snow

Ice is formed by the breath of God, and watery
expanses are frozen. He saturates clouds with
moisture . . . They swirl about, turning round
and round at His direction, accomplishing
everything He commands them over the surface of
the inhabited world.

—Job 37:10–12

"No snow," my son said when he awoke early one December morning and pulled back the curtains to check out our suburban Atlanta yard. "It must be Christmastime."

He was right. Around here nobody needs a calendar to know when Christmas is getting close. He could tell from the typically balmy weather, which forced us to dress in our usual clothing for that time of year: lightweight pants and short-sleeved shirts. If the temperature had risen a little more, we might have broken out the sandals and sunscreen too.

While most of the country is usually frosted as snowy white as a wedding cake by mid-December, here in the Deep South, no snow is our tradition. I can't remember how many holiday mornings we've hopped out of bed to celebrate Christmas Day and open gifts around the tree while the outside temperature shot past sixty degrees. .

I always like to wear my red, candy-cane striped apron when I cook our Christmas turkey for lunch, but I usually have to ditch my dressy pants to wear shorts beneath it, and it's our routine to flick on the air conditioning to beat back the humidity as the house starts to fill with guests.

Not for us Southern ladies, those pretty winter sweaters made of wool or mohair and decorated with reindeer and elves. Forget the Yule log burning merrily in the hearth. Toasty Christmases, I'm sorry to say, are predictable here, as common as the grimace on the face of a mall Santa Claus by the end of shopping season.

I suppose only other Southerners can understand this, but those of us who were born and raised below the Mason-Dixon Line harbor a secret wish to see the white stuff. It doesn't matter that our Northern friends stare in horror when I yearn out loud for snowdrifts to jump in or the sparkle of icicles hanging from the roof. They've smacked their foreheads in disbelief plenty of times as they argue that icy weather means nothing more than banks of dirty, plowed snow. Those killjoys like to annoy me by saying that salt, spread over the highways to combat all that glorious snow, will bounce up into the wheel wells of my car every time I pull out of my driveway, where eventually it will rime the undercarriage and rust holes in the metal. I'm still not budging. They can play Scrooge all they want, but they can't even scare me with tales of freezing weather that runs from Labor Day into the next July.

I've seen those greeting cards dusted with silvery glitter, and I've watched the movies with jingle-belled horses dashing up and over white slopes, and I want snow. I like to tell the naysayers, just throw in some hot chocolate, warm mittens, and a pair of sturdy boots for stomping around in the snowy woods, and I'll be in heaven.

This is when most people shake their heads and walk away, convinced they can't argue with a madwoman.

I know, I know: I wouldn't *really* want snowdrifts that pile over the rooftop and blanket the windows of the house, or a glaze of thick, black ice that leaves the streets impassable and treacherous, but think of it this way: Snow does have a purpose and a good reason for being.

Rain and snow, the Lord says in the book of Isaiah, are sent from heaven to saturate the earth, to make it "germinate and sprout . . . providing seed to sow and food to eat" (55:10). Every farmer knows that when spring returns, meltwater feeds our rivers and streams, providing water for crops in the field. Snow, even if it does strand your school-age kids at home sometimes, is another part of God's provision for us.

In the Bible snow often serves as a sign of God's power, too. As Job's friends remind him: "For He says to the snow, 'Fall to the earth,' and the torrential rains, His mighty torrential rains, serve as His signature to all mankind, so that all men may know His work" (Job 37:6–7). And, the men add, imagine the icy treasure-house where that snow is stored!

Many wonders, like that treasure-house, are hidden from our sight until something miraculous happens, like a rare snow day here in the South. Then God reveals his majesty in an infinite diversity of snowflakes that swirl out of the sky. What you've heard about no two snowflakes being exactly alike is true, according to Kenneth G. Libbrecht, a Cal Tech physicist, at least until you get down to a mind-boggling molecular level, where all electrons, the elementary particles that I think of as God's building blocks, are basically identical. Even then, Libbrecht says that the odds of two snowflakes having the same molecular layout in the "lifetime of the Universe" is so small, it is "indistinguishable from zero."[17]

Why would God do this? Why create a unique shape for each and every new snowflake that falls? Does God really need so many different kinds of ice crystals, like the ones Libbrecht categorizes as simple prisms, fernlike stellar dendrites, split plates and stars, needles, and hollows?

I can only conclude that God freezes snow and ice into endlessly beautiful new forms simply because he can and because he delights in giving us something to marvel over every winter. I don't think snow was just created for our food and water supply; I also believe God stirred in some fun, making it useful for sledding and skiing, for packing snowballs in backyard battles, or for simply admiring from a chair in the warm house.

Just as the snow is a source of life and joy for us, God also sent Jesus to give us new life and hope. If we're honest, we measure the width and depth of our transgressions and admit that we all fall short. Our hearts, no matter how hard we try to keep them pure, are as stained and filthy as snow plowed from the dirty street. We are all sinners, in need of forgiveness and salvation, like David, who beseeched God, "Purify me with hyssop, and I will be clean; wash me, and I will be whiter than snow. . . . Turn Your face away from my sins and blot out all my guilt" (Ps. 51:7, 9). God has done that; he makes us clean again through Jesus' sacrifice on the cross.

Remember how the angels appeared to the shepherds watching over their flock one night, announcing tidings of great joy at the birth of God's own Son? In spite of the words we sing in traditional Christmas carols, we don't know if Jesus was really born on a cold night, when snow lay on the ground, but that scene would have been appropriate. Snow brings us joy; Jesus came in joy too.

When we do get a rare and beautiful snow day in my part of the South, everything changes. Our schools shut down and Department of Transportation trucks crank up before dawn to pour sand and melting compound over streets glazed with black, invisible, dangerous ice. The landscape is transformed as the olive-drab evergreens start to sparkle with icy flakes. There's an excitement here as we rush to grocery stores to buy bread and extra milk, as if this storm could shut businesses down for days (and a few of our snowstorms have done that). Our kids look at it as a great escape from school; most of us adults consider it an escape from work. We go outside to slide on snowy hills with them, using sheets of cardboard, cookie pans, trash can lids, or whatever we can turn into a sled at a moment's notice.

Like any event that forces us to slow down for a while and step out of our daily routine, a snow day can also become a spiritual experience. If we're not dragged outside to help build a snowman with a carrot nose and twiggy arms, it's a good opportunity to spend quiet time in prayer. Snow has an insulating quality, and when it mounds over yards and trees and buildings, it brings a strange hush to the world. You can hear a lot of sounds then that are usually lost in the cacophony of everyday life. Even God's voice is a little easier to perceive when there's not much competing noise.

I love the Bible verses about snow, when God reasons with us—not so unlike the friends who try to reason me out of my snow fantasies.

"'Come, let us discuss this,' says the LORD. 'Though your sins are like scarlet, they will be as white as snow; though they are as red as crimson, they will be like wool. If you are willing and obedient . . .'" (Isa. 1:18–19).

You can't miss a kid out playing in the snow, dressed in a red jacket, or a flock of bright red cardinals feasting on sunflower seeds at a winter feeder. Red is a shocking contrast on a pure, pristine background. Our sins stand out that boldly, too, against the sinlessness of Jesus. Only our obedience through baptism and belief can erase the scarlet stains of our transgressions, washing us clean as a sprinkle of fresh flakes, leaving us pleasing and acceptable to God.

I want snow; I can't help it, even though I seldom see it. When I'm forced to be realistic, I know snow means soaring utility bills and busted water pipes, slick roads and traffic accidents, frostbite and heart-pounding path shoveling. But I prefer my dream of evergreens decorated with sugary flakes and bare branches glittering with ice. I like to hear the little stream behind our house gurgling under a crystallized layer of snow and watch the squirrels showering snowflakes to the ground with every leap from tree to tree. I like rolling a snowball and catching my unsuspecting neighbor at his mailbox, even if he sneak-attacks me back later.

Snow doesn't come my way very often, but I'm patient. I'll wait. Until the weatherman predicts another snowfall, I'll be content with thanking the One who sends it and the Son who washes away our blame. "Praise the LORD from the earth . . . lightning and hail, snow and cloud" (Ps. 148:7–8).

Streetlight Dog

I think God will have prepared everything for our perfect happiness. If it takes my dog being there [in heaven], I believe he'll be there.

—Billy Graham

wise person once said, "You have to take all the dogs God gives you." Not everybody is willing to take in every mutt or mongrel that shows up, uninvited, on your doorstep, but the person who made that statement sounds a lot like some good-hearted friends of mine I'll call Jack and Martha. The couple lives in a neat double-wide trailer on about a dozen acres in rural Alabama, and when you drive out to see them, you have to bump and rumble down a winding dirt road to get to their place. The nearest neighbors are around the next bend, not right next door, so at night, it's pretty dark and quiet all around.

Sometimes, after they've flicked off the TV and gone to bed, they'll be awakened by the sound of a car slowing down in front of the row of mailboxes that serves several homes in the area. A moment later they'll hear the sound of a door slamming shut, and then a car engine revving as the midnight visitor speeds away.

When they get up the next morning, Jack and Martha know what they'll find when they head out to their mailbox with the day's first cup of coffee in hand. Without fail, someone will have dumped out a poor, old dog with a mangy coat, or left a card-board box filled with hungry puppies on their property.

Now, my friends have dogs already—a couple of spoiled indoor Chihuahuas that cuddle next to Martha on the bed at night and a couple of old-fashioned yard dogs that prefer to stay outside so they can bark at a passing coyote and howl at the moon when they feel like it. Jack and Martha also are the proud owners of a bunch of barn cats, a sweet little mare, and a gaggle of laying chickens in a coop, so their wallets already take a hit from buying animal food and paying vet bills.

But you can probably guess what they do when they find the latest castoff on their doorstep; they just sigh and take in some-body else's problem. They'll ask around until they find good homes for the pups, but for the aging or ailing dogs that nobody else wants, they make a bed on a spare blanket and see that they get soft food for their old teeth or do whatever else is needed to keep their newest four-legged companion comfortable and happy for as long as it takes. They give those throw-away dogs the same loving care any kennel club pedigreed pet would get, because their hearts are big, even if their bank account isn't.

Some people call them suckers for taking in abandoned animals; the rest of us just love them like crazy. The way that Jack and Martha respond to need, and the way they step up to the plate when someone or something is in trouble, embodies the love that Jesus wants us all to show to the unwanted, unwashed, and unloved.

I've got to admit I've always felt a calling to take all the dogs God sends me too. Sometimes I've even set out to bring them home on purpose.

I first spotted the dog we would eventually name Red when I drove home through my neighborhood one late fall evening. The streetlights had already blinked on, even though the sky still held some light, and as I turned the last corner to my house, out of the corner of my eye, I noticed something sitting next to the light post, huddled close to the fire hydrant.

I did a double take. Out of curiosity, because our county has a strict leash law, I turned around to go back and take another look at what I suspected was a stray. Sure enough, a handsome, reddish-brown dog—a big, rough-looking mix, I'd figure out later—was curled in the dry, brown grass. An empty can, about the size that tuna fish and cat food came in, sat on its side near him, as if he'd licked it clean and knocked it over. There was also a greasy-looking paper plate nearby.

My heart sank. I realized that a kind soul had already figured out this doggy was homeless and hungry, and he or she had put out some food and water to see him through the blistering hot day. We'd been enduring a spell of brutal hot weather, even though summer had passed. That evening, the temperature had yet to drop below ninety degrees, and the humidity was stifling.

I pulled up to the curb, some distance from the dog, and parked. I love animals, but I know enough not to approach a stray that might be inclined to bite me. The dog stood up when I walked a little closer, as if he was alarmed at my approach, but he stayed put.

I squatted down, staying near my car in case I had to jump back in, and called to him in my softest, library-type voice. He ventured a little closer, and then a little more. I sidled closer too. Yes, the paper plate showed signs of having held some kind of pet food, and the can, even on its side, showed a glimmer of water.

I couldn't get the dog to come closer, but I could see that he didn't have a collar, so I hopped back in the car and drove home to fetch more food and more water. The tin can had been too small to hold enough for such a big guy to drink, I told myself, and how long ago had he eaten the food?

I fed and watered my new friend that night, and every night thereafter for that week, and the week after and the week after. He would never let me get close enough to touch him, although he gobbled up the food and lapped the water and seemed willing to take any leftovers we had from the table. Sometimes I drove by in the afternoons and didn't see him near the hydrant, and my heart jumped, half with hope that he'd gone back to wherever he had come from, and half-alarmed that he had run out onto a busy road or wandered into the woods that surround our neighborhood and gotten lost.

On nights I didn't see him at the first fire hydrant, I'd drive around and around, until I eventually found him under another streetlight that had a fire hydrant at its base. I could only wonder if he was seeking out light on dark evenings, or if he somehow associated a hydrant with where he belonged—perhaps he'd been tied to one all the time and had gotten free, but still thought he was supposed to lie beside it. Was he drawn to the light because it represented safety and security to him, or the hydrant because he'd been leashed to one, and didn't even know how to live without a cruel boundary?

As the days rolled past, people started to notice the crazy woman—that would be me—obsessed with the stray dog, which was Red. A couple of times, other neighbors came by to offer fresh water and canned food for him. Once a sweet girl who lived up the street opened a tin of cat food and helped me coax Red into her fenced backyard. We thought if we could corral him, we could calm him down long enough for me to put a leash on him and take him home with me. No such luck. We got him into her yard, quietly shut the gate behind him, and he immediately seemed to know he was trapped. He bolted and jumped the fence on the far side of her yard, escaping from us the rest of the night, no matter how much more deliciously fishy-smelling food we offered.

But the next night I found Red beside yet another nearby fire hydrant/streetlight combination, and he seemed happy to see me. I started trying to lead him back to my house, and over and over I'd lead home with me, block by block, literally yard by yard, dropping bites of yummy food from my fingers and urging him to trail behind me. I hoped that if I could get him in my yard, eventually I could tame him enough to come inside, or at least live within our fence, where he'd be safe and loved. You would've thought he knew my street address though. After following me for almost a mile every time, he'd get within a few hundred feet of my front porch and turn and trot away.

I felt desperate for a long time, fearful that he'd get run over or picked up and taken to the pound if someone didn't give him a home. Yet how do you give a home to someone who doesn't want one?

I tried a new tactic. Night after night I brought his food and just sat quietly on the ground nearby, not moving, as he ate. When he settled back down around his hydrant of the night, I'd inch closer and closer. After a while I'd place my hand on the ground near him. Once I finally reached out cautiously and touched his back. Startled, he jumped and ran. But the next day and the next I tried again, and eventually he let me pat him, gently stroking his ears and back. Finally he trusted me enough to even rest his big, beautiful head on my legs.

One evening I brought a collar and leash in my pocket and slipped it out while Red dozed in my lap. Gently I put it around his neck and stood up, hoping to lead him home, but he awoke and fought against my gentle tugs like a bucking bronco. Horrified and ashamed that I'd violated his trust, I tore the leash off as fast as I could. "I'm so sorry, Red," I called after him as he ran away. "I only wanted to help. I'll never do that again."

I never did try to force Red to do anything again, but I knew our days had to be numbered. How long could I track him every night, since he insisted on wandering from hydrant to hydrant around our big neighborhood? A couple of joggers told me once that they'd seen him in other subdivisions. "He must wander all over the county," one of them said, and I knew if he left my area, I'd probably never be able to find him again.

I started to get a reputation in the neighborhood without realizing it. One night when I was busy with a chore, I asked my son to take Red's food up the street, where I'd seen the dog earlier in the day. While Michael stood waiting for Red to wolf down his dinner, a neighbor drove up. "Some lady is out here every night," the man said, "trying to coax that dog to go home with her. Just thought you should know. Don't try to do anything with him. That lady wants him."

Michael grinned. "I know," he told the helpful neighbor. "That lady's my mom."

Too soon our fair, dry weather ended. At the end of autumn, the rains came, and some nights I couldn't find Red at all and was left to hope he'd crawled under someone's porch or found thick brush to sleep under.

Then one night Red was nowhere to be found. I looked all that evening and sent my husband and son to drive around too. We went into an adjacent neighborhood, calling and whistling, holding tins of that smelly, fishy cat food that I knew he loved. I called the pound every day for a week, describing him and begging the workers to let me know if one of their trucks rounded him up and turned him in.

It hurts my heart to say that I never saw Red again. I wanted to help him.

But what happened that summer, under those streetlights, gave me insight into how God also pursues us when we go wandering and get lost. And lots of us do get lost, even people who have been raised in churches and taught about the Bible and Jesus on the cross.

With all life throws at us, it's not that hard sometimes to get separated from our Father, and wind up suspicious and mistrustful of anybody who tries to approach us on his behalf. Some people are just plain scared, because they've been misused, hurt, or abandoned. Others are fearful, not sure why anybody would show an interest in them, lacking the confidence to believe they're worth the effort, or deserving of God's attention.

Because I was the pursuer in Red's case, rather than the pursued, I could also imagine, in some small way, how Jesus must feel when we reject him. He offers his unconditional love and the promise of eternal life, yet we bolt, running as hard as we can in the opposite direction, not even knowing what it is we're running toward. Just running, blindly.

Thanks to grace and mercy, Jesus doesn't give up. He keeps searching for us no matter how far we stray or how vigorously we fight against him, and there's a celebration in heaven when even one of us comes home. What boundless love, to follow us forever, if that's what it takes to redeem a heart!

Because God created animals and placed them in the Garden of Eden as companions to Adam and Eve, I believe he loves them. He keeps his eye on the sparrow; he makes the fish multiply in the sea; he adorns the horse with its thick mane and numbers the days until the mountain goats give birth, as he reminds us in the book of Job. One day, we're told, the Creator will even cause the lion to lie down beside the lamb, in a world where peace rules and sin is vanquished.

I'm grateful to have had Red in my life, if only for a little while, and I ask God to take care of him. I try to pray, as Dr. Albert Schweitzer wrote in his book *Memoirs of Childhood and Youth*, "Dear God, protect and bless all beings that breathe, keep all evil from them, and let them sleep in peace."[18] Amen.

Resurrection in the Garden

*Our Lord has written the promise of
resurrection, not in books alone,
but in every leaf in springtime.*

—Martin Luther

*P*erhaps because I'm a person who loves the earth and all the flowers and fruits and, yes, even some of the weeds that spring up from it, I like to think that Jesus also had a deep love for the natural world. After all, when he needed a quiet place to go, knowing his death was close at hand, Jesus sought out a garden across the Kidron Valley at Gethsemane near the Mount of Olives, where he asked his disciples to sit some distance away so he could kneel and pray to his Father.

Scholars say that Gethsemane is Greek for the Hebrew phrase that meant "oil press," which suggests that the garden was the site of an olive farm or grove.[19] It's easy to imagine that the men visited there because they could recline on the ground under the shade to talk and rest, maybe even laugh and share with the Master. Whether they met in the evenings to enjoy the cool of the day, or just after sunrise when they would have heard the music of birdsong in the early morning hours, the garden would have been a lovely place, soothing to both spirit and mind.

Jesus went to Gethsemane for the last time to find peace, as he struggled with the task that lay before him. In his anguish, as he prayed and asked his Father to spare him, if that was possible, an angel appeared to minister to him and help him find the strength to carry out God's plan for our salvation.

After his crucifixion, the first place Jesus appeared in resurrected form was, once again, in a garden. In fact, when Mary Magdalene first saw the risen Lord, she didn't even recognize him and mistook him for the gardener. How appropriate, that Mary found Jesus in the very place where life returns every spring as tender, green leaves shoot up out of the earth and flowers unfold their shy blossoms.

Earlier in his ministry Jesus had told his followers that God was the keeper of the vineyard, and he was the true vine. God prunes back the branches that don't yield fruit, he told them, which is necessary to make the branches more fruitful and abundant. "Remain in Me, and I in you. Just as a branch is unable to produce fruit by itself unless it remains on the vine, so neither can you unless you remain in Me" (John 15:4).

Just before Jesus died, while he suffered in obedience on the cross, Jesus spoke to one of the criminals hanging on a cross beside him. The man had asked Jesus to remember him when he came into his kingdom. "I assure you," Jesus replied, "Today you will be with Me in paradise" (Luke 23:43).

The American author E. B. White, best known for his beloved children's books *Charlotte's Web* and *Stuart Little*, once described how his wife, Katharine, near the end of her long struggle with cancer, went into her garden with a sketch she'd drawn for planting bulbs. He said she behaved as if "there would be yet another spring," even knowing her time was short, as she sat there "under those dark skies in the dying October, calmly plotting the resurrection."[20]

Katharine, who was a writer like her husband, was also a longtime gardener, so perhaps she was able to approach the end calmly because she knew from experience that what is committed to the ground can live again. She would have known that the papery-shelled bulbs she tucked into the dirt and the tiny seeds she scattered over the ground would be fed by the rain until one day, newborn plants would push through the earth and turn their faces to the sun.

For a gardener, growing something beautiful from an unassuming bulb or a gnarled tuber often feels mysterious. We hoe and dig, we pull (and pull) the weeds, we apply a little fertilizer here and a little mulch there, and if we're lucky, we wind up with a nice garden. But we know, in the end, that we didn't actually create the rose that bloomed from a cutting, or form the tomatoes that sprang up from seeds. We only tend the plants. It's God who makes them grow, and who brings them out of the dark ground and into the light.

As believers, we take great comfort and joy in the promise of a resurrection, because we know Jesus conquered death and the darkness of the grave.

When Martha grieved for her dead brother, Lazarus, Jesus assured her, "Your brother will rise again" (John 11:23). Then, "Jesus said to her, 'I am the resurrection and the life. The one who believes in Me, even if he dies, will live. Everyone who lives and believes in Me will never die—ever. Do you believe this?'" (John 11:25).

That's the big question, isn't it? Do you believe?

"Yes," Martha answered, "I believe." When I read that passage, I often wonder how Martha looked when she spoke those words. Did she drop to her knees in awe and reverence for God's power? Did she shout the words joyfully, her face upturned and her hands lifted in praise? Did her tears flow as she heard Jesus' wonderful promise and felt overcome with gratitude for mercy and grace?

"Yes," Martha said, "I believe." Her words still echo: we believe, too, and the resurrection we anticipate allows us to live every ordinary, passing day with hope in our hearts and peace for our minds.

God has given us a beautiful garden, this natural world, in which to grow and flourish.

But through his Son, he invites us to an eternal life that

makes even the most glorious physical life—the only kind we know, in our limited understanding—seem shabby and poor.

Do you believe? My prayer is that your answer, like Martha's, is yes. May you always be blessed by God's tender mercies and rest in his perfect peace.

"Surely goodness and mercy shall follow me all the days of my life: and I will dwell in the house of the LORD for ever" (Ps. 23:6 KJV).

Study Guide/Discussion Questions

Introduction

We all know that it's a good idea to see a doctor regularly for a physical, or what's commonly called a checkup. That's how we catch and correct a lot of problems that have a way of creeping up on us, like high blood pressure or a vitamin deficiency.

It's also wise to take time for a spiritual checkup now and then, to assess where we are in relationship with God and to determine whether the way we're living our lives truly reflects our faith.

So how is your heart—your spiritual heart? Are you living with an "attitude of gratitude," even in, or especially in, difficult circumstances? If your spiritual heart feels a little weak and your attitude needs work, don't despair. Remember that the Scriptures tell us that God's grace is enough; his power is revealed most gloriously when we are weak.

Little Mercies is all about finding the gems in the rubble. We can't always change our circumstances, but we can learn to revel in God's grace and goodness and sweeten our ordinary, daily lives with the honey of his Word and his love.

To get started, read Philippians 4:4–6 for Paul's advice on cultivating joy in your life. Now read Philippians 4:7. What did Paul promise we'll receive, if we do these things? That's something to give thanks for right now. Take a moment to praise and thank God for his gifts.

Chapter 1

Wildlife rehabilitators like Monteen McCord have tough jobs. When they try to help injured or orphaned creatures, they can end up bitten, clawed, or worse. If they're paid at all, the money seldom goes far enough to cover medicines, vet bills, and food. And as for becoming famous or well-known—can you name anyone who does this kind of work? (Don't count celebrities on TV. We're talking about ordinary folks.)

Lots of other people do the same kind of underpaid, under appreciated, difficult tasks. Think about the challenges many of today's teachers face, for example, or nursing home assistants or court-appointed advocates for abused children. Why do any of them persevere?

God pours his grace out over our sinful lives, yet often we stumble in our walk of faith again and again. Why does he persevere with us?

How do you define *grace*? Is it an abstract concept that suggests God's unmerited, unearned favor in your life, or can you think of concrete examples?

Finally, imagine how it must feel to love and nurture a broken creature, and then to give it the choice to leave or stay with you. Rhonda, the hawk Monteen tended so carefully, flew away without a backward glance. Sometimes we take our eyes off the God who restores and heals us, too, but does that change the grace he shows us? Read John 1:14–17. Isn't that something to celebrate?

Chapter 2

Read Romans 8:18–23. According to the Scripture, creation was held fast in the bonds of corruption until, groaning like a woman in labor, it was set free through redemption in Jesus Christ. Now read Luke 19:37, which tells us that when Jesus rode into Jerusalem on a donkey, "the whole crowd of the disciples began to praise God joyfully with a loud voice." Look back at the verse and pick out the word that describes *how* the crowd praised God. Without Jesus, the world groans. With him, we praise God joyfully.

What can you praise God for today? Consider the natural world around us, and thank him for something small that you've seen today, something that you would usually overlook. What do such wonderful, tiny things reveal about the One who created them? Does that give you more confidence in the care and concern he has for you?

Chapter 3

Did you ever go fishing and come home with an empty creel or ice chest? Read John 10:10, in which Jesus said he came to give us life in abundance. Abundance literally means an ample supply or an overflowing fullness—but of what? The fishermen in Jesus' time needed a big catch of fresh fish to provide for their families, but what do you need or want, in order to have an abundant life? (Think about the difference between *want* and *need* when you answer.) Once you've pinned down exactly what is most important in your life, stop to count up all God has given you. Now rethink that ice chest. Is it as empty as you thought?

Today we share bread and the cup in remembrance of Jesus, a practice we call Communion. In a broader, worldly sense, communion is also the act of sharing feelings and thoughts. Read Hebrews 10:25, which tells believers not to stay away from meetings and to encourage one another. How can you commune with others, so that you share not only your thoughts and feelings, but the presence of our living Lord?

Chapter 4

Whether you work in a cubicle or an oil rig in the middle of an ocean, whether you're a stay-at-home mom or an astronaut, you have a job, something you do each day, or something you're responsible for. How do you feel about your work?

Thoreau once said that most of us live lives of quiet desperation, meaning that most of us go about our day-to-day affairs out of duty or necessity but without enthusiasm or happiness. That's probably true, unfortunately, but the story doesn't have to end with drudgery.

How can you perform your job, whether you're caring for an ailing, forgetful parent or engineering a new machine in some way that will serve the Lord and glorify his name? Can you sing behind your plow/desk/cash register and thank the One who provides for you? Read Psalm 33:2–4 and put some gladness in your song.

Chapter 5

If you ask enough people, you'll probably find at least one or two who say they've seen an angel. In biblical times, angels frequently appeared and performed many different tasks, such as announcing Jesus's birth, or protecting people from harm, like the angel who walked with Daniel and his friends in the fiery furnace. Angels visited Paul with a message of encouragement when he and his fellow sailors thought their ship might wreck on the rocks, leaving them all to drown in the sea, and angels delivered a poor beggar named Lazarus straight to Abraham's side when he died (Luke 16:22).

But sometimes we forget that we, ourselves, can act like angels. We can encourage others with our words and actions. We can announce the Good News to those who haven't heard it, and we can live it out for those who have heard it but haven't really seen it practiced. Most of us will never be able to say we've actually saved someone's life, but there are ways we can help and serve, and we can trust God to do what we cannot.

Brody and Kristi ministered to others, even when they seemed to be on the receiving end, by sharing their faith, their hope, and their sweet spirits. When Brody passed away, his doctors, nurses, and friends turned out to celebrate his life, and then went right back to work in their hospitals and pediatric wards, more determined than ever to help the next child who came along.

How can you be an "angel" in someone else's life, reflecting God's love, grace, and goodness, even though you don't have wings?

Chapter 6

There's a little more to the story about hiking with the llamas than you just read. Remember that I mentioned the high elevation? We were climbing in the Taos, New Mexico, area, where the air changes in density because of the city's high elevation. It becomes thinner and less oxygen-rich, which it means that people who live much closer to sea level, like me, have to breathe harder when we're exercising or even walking and hiking—much harder.

I made it down the winding, switchback path just fine, but getting back up was altogether different. I kept having to stop and gasp for air; I felt extremely fatigued, and no matter how hard I breathed, my lungs couldn't seem to take in enough oxygen. Soon I fell behind in the line of hikers and llamas, and I wound up being the last person to make it back to the top.

Stuart Wilde, bless him, did what every good guide does: He dropped behind to stay with me. He didn't leave my side until I was safely out, even though he was perfectly fine and could have sprinted to the finish (where everybody else was already) if he'd wanted to.

But the best, most trustworthy guides don't do that. They don't leave anyone behind, especially the ones struggling to make it. They stay; they abide. They're patient and encouraging and they rejoice when you finally achieve your goal.

Talk about a few of the "guides" in the Bible that God sent to people who were struggling or in need. When the going got tough, how did they offer encouragement and support? Where did their strength come from?

Have you ever found yourself off track, or falling behind, and in need of a guide? Did you feel God's presence, or did he send someone or something to get you on your way again? Is it possible that even small things, like a cup of water in a desert place, can make a difference in times of trouble? If the answer is yes, stop and give thanks to our Father for small gifts!

Chapter 7

In the play *Our Town*, Emily can hardly bear to look back at even an ordinary day in her past life, because she finally realizes how precious each seemingly ordinary day really was. Talk about an ordinary day in your life, and explore the little gems of grace that it contained.

If you have a camera, or if you can borrow one, take a quick field trip. Walk around and spend time just looking through the lens, sharpening its focus, and observing. Are there rainbow colors in the soap bubbles when you're washing dishes? Is there a tiny forest of green moss growing under a shady tree outside? Can you work on noticing more details so you can better appreciate the Maker of heaven and earth?

Express your thanks for this day we've been given, and then take the time you need to really enjoy living it!

Chapter 8

I was sorry to find a dead bee in my windowsill recently. Evidently it became trapped in the house, and I didn't find it in time to raise the screen and help it find its way out. (I don't want to get stung, of course, but I'd rather see a bee go home to its hive, where it can accomplish the good work of making honey, than kill it.)

Honey is mentioned a number of times in the Scriptures. It's not only a wholesome food, it's also used as a medicine and exchanged as a valuable gift. Jesus ate broiled fish and a honeycomb, given to him by his disciples, when he appeared to them after his resurrection (see Luke 24:41–42). It's possible, some scholars say, that the heaven-sent manna provided to the

Israelites as they wandered in the desert was actually honeydew; at least we know it tasted as sweet as honey. The Bible also mentions mixing wine with honey; Jacob sent honey as a gift when he sent his son to Egypt to meet with the governor; and in both Ezekiel 3:3 and Revelation 10:9–10, there are accounts of men being instructed to eat books that taste as sweet as that golden syrup. Clearly honey was important in biblical times, and it symbolized the goodness of taking God's Word into our lives.

In ancient times collecting honey was no easy task. It's still tricky for modern-day beekeepers, who risk getting stung despite their protective gear and smokers. Do their efforts to collect honey tell you something about its value?

What have people sacrificed to receive or acquire the Word of God? Don't limit your discussion to ancient history; consider what modern people in other countries must do.

How does the Bible nourish and enrich your life today? What do you have to do to read the Word? When you compare what you have to do to what people in other lands go through to taste the sweetness of God's words, do you see a blessing to be thankful for?

Chapter 9

Read the story of the prodigal son in Luke 15:11–32. Here is a story of great forgiveness in spite of great disobedience, but look closely at the words that describe how the father greeted his son. The man ran out to meet him, embraced the boy in his rags and filth, and lavished kisses on him. Three times he told his son they were going to celebrate his homecoming, and there was music, dancing, and rejoicing.

Have you ever been in a position to grant forgiveness? Were you able to give it joyfully?

Think about a time when you've gone to God to confess a sin and ask for grace. How did it feel? Your heart should be filled with happiness to know that you're forgiven when you ask. Better still, read Psalm 103:10–12, and see what happens to sin when you repent. Now, thank your Father for his perfect and unconditional love!

Chapter 10

Some people feel a rush of exhilaration when they try something entirely new and daring, like flying in a small plane, skiing down a mountainside, or parachuting into a blue sky. Others—and this includes me—like to have our feet fixed firmly on the ground. If we're forced to launch ourselves into some strange and risky venture, we tend to white-knuckle it all the way.

But it shouldn't be that way when we plant our feet firmly in matters of faith. Sure, feeling excited is fine—but fear needs to come out of our vocabulary if we're really trusting our lives to God.

In terms of earthly adventures, what's the scariest thing you've ever done? What's the biggest risk you've taken in spiritual matters? How did things turn out, and what did the whole experience teach you about the nature of God?

Chapter 11

Readers, I hope the little story of Bob the egg gave you a laugh. Doctors say that laughter brings oxygen into our lungs, lowers the blood pressure, and relieves stress, and we certainly know that it's good for the spirit. Take a look at these verses to see what the Bible says about laughter and joy—Psalm 126:2–3; Proverbs 17:22; Genesis 21:6; and Job 8:21.

Some days it's hard to laugh at anything, especially when bills flood our mailboxes, beloved pets pass away, and illnesses unexpectedly change our lives. You'd think that only kids could laugh when times get tough. But remember, Jesus wants us to have the hearts and faith of children, as he indicated in Matthew 18:2–4. No hard shells—that is, no hard hearts—for believers!

As for our egos—that word is only one letter away from the word *egg*, and both can be pretty fragile. Read God's command about humility in Colossians 3:12. The world preaches a strong message nowadays about asserting oneself, not "taking anything off of anybody," and so forth, and, yes, it's good to have self-respect and strong values. But God's people don't have to act hard-boiled to know who they are and whom they serve. Soft hearts are more open to finding joy even in the smallest, most simple things.

Have you ever felt cracked or broken? Could you find any joy or laughter in your circumstances? If not, did you look for it in the right place—in the hope we have through Jesus? The next time life drops you from the heights, remember that it's not the strength of your shell that cushions and protects you. It's the strength of your God.

Chapter 12

Stripped of his dignity and clothing, pursued by hostile natives, surrounded by other-worldly sights, sounds, and smells from bubbling mud pots and smoking cones, John Colter must have felt lost indeed. But suppose his run through the wilderness had never happened. We would have been the losers—at least, until someone else discovered the pristine, savage beauty that would become Yellowstone, our first national park.

Think about a wilderness you've been through, whether it's a literal one, like a desert or overgrown forest, or a figurative one, like a devastating heartbreak or failure of faith. Did you see anything of value there? Even if you didn't discover anything useful at the time, can you look back and see anything the experience gave you or taught you in the long run?

In 1988 a tremendous fire roared through Yellowstone, the largest wildfire in the park's recorded history, burning into the very ground so deeply that some foresters predicted that even seeds lying dormant would be destroyed. The fire raged for months, until cool, moist weather finally arrived that fall and extinguished the flames. There would be no plants that next year, scientists said sadly; it would take years and years before anything could sprout after such devastation.

But guess what? The foresters were wrong. Plants quickly reappeared at the base of tall, blackened trees. It turned out that Yellowstone actually benefited from the big fire, which cleared the land and let smaller plant species emerge.

What does that suggest to you? Can you remember being in a dangerous or desperate situation—whether it was a physical place or a spiritual or emotional one? Did your journey, however unexpected or unwanted at the time, lead you to something bigger, deeper, or even better? If it didn't, don't despair. God isn't finished with any of us yet!

Chapter 13

Is there a loaf of store-bought bread sitting at home on your counter right now? There's one on mine. It's a pretty humble, homely-looking thing, flopping around in its plastic bag, and if I don't use it fast enough, soon it's sprouting those nasty gray-green whiskers that signal mold is beginning to grow.

Plain old white bread, the kind most of us eat, doesn't look like much until you slather it with some mayo and spicy mustard, add a few crisp lettuce leaves and tomato slices, stack it with yummy deli slices, and serve it up for a sandwich.

But think about it: The whole world needs bread, and ordinary bread is the substance Jesus chose to describe himself. Why do you think he chose it? What did he want us to realize?

Have you ever made your own bread? It can be a lot of work, kneading the sticky dough and shaping the loaves. Add too much flour, and you've baked a brick; leave it in the oven too long, and the burned smell permeates your house. But is it an art worth teaching to the next generation? Why? What gets lost if we don't pass on our knowledge? What other things should we teach our children?

Chapter 14

Where you live probably determines how you feel about snow. If you're a Southerner, like me, you can't get enough of the fluffy stuff, because it's rare and beautiful around here. If you're from the North, where you drive through dirty slush piled along the roadsides for months and pay exorbitant heating bills when drifts pile up around your windows—well, I wouldn't like that either.

But for the moment, let's think about references to snow in the Bible. According to the Word, its whiteness covers the stain of sin. Why do you think the Bible describes sin as crimson-colored or red?

Interestingly, just as different people have different feelings about snow, the wintry stuff has a mixed symbolism in the Word. In Exodus 4:6 and Numbers 12:10, the diseased skin of leprosy is said to look as white as snow—that's pretty negative.

In other passages the whiteness of snow symbolizes purity and cleanliness. What does snow represent to you?

One other intriguing thing about snow in the Bible is that it signals the power of God, who commands all the elements of the earth; read Job 38:22, for an example of this reality. While scientists say that snowflakes may look alike, it's true, to some degree, that no two snowflakes have exactly the same structure. Imagine how much variety there must be in a single cup of fallen snow! Why do you think God makes each snowflake different? Is he revealing his glory and infinite care and concern, even in the tiny ice crystals that quickly melt and disappear? Thank him for the grace that he sprinkles from the winter sky as snow!

Chapter 15

I still miss Red, the elusive, homeless dog who lived under first one streetlight and then another in my neighborhood. I tried to earn his trust, but apparently he'd been too misused to warm up to me. When you can't use words to communicate, you hope gestures and actions will serve, but sometimes, if mistrust and pain run too deep, even those are not enough.

I see a lot of "Reds" among us, people too wounded, physically, emotionally, or spiritually, to take love even when it's freely given. Maybe that explains why some of us can't or won't accept the grace and salvation Jesus offers. What's the best thing we can do, when we try to reconcile or bring someone to the Lord, and that person runs away from our help?

I grew discouraged when Red didn't respond to my help, and I grieved when he finally disappeared. But does God ever give up when one of his frightened, hurt children is in need? The answer, of course, is no—praise him!

Chapter 16

Think about Katharine White. Knowing her death was imminent, she planted a garden anyway, confident that what was committed to the ground would reappear in time, even if she wasn't there to see and enjoy it.

Read John 11:25. Knowing what you know, can you share Katharine's confidence? What a blessing, to live under grace, forgiven!

Notes

1. See http://www.imdb.com/title/tt0054885.
2. See http://www.imdb.com/title/tt0089457.
3. See http://www.movie-locations.com/movies/r/riverruns.html.
4. See http://www.flyfishinghistory.com/dame.htm and http://www.fly-fishingjoy.com/Fly_Fishing_History.html.
5. See www.folkschool.com, "Campbell, John C. and Olive Dame," *Encyclopedia of Appalachia,* edited by Rudy Anderson and Jean Haskell, 2006.
6. Mack Secord, interview with author, August 21, 2009, and http://www.aircareall.org.
7. "Hold On," Scott Johnson, composer and words set to music by the group Joymasters.
8. Wild Earth Llama Adventures, operated by Stuart Wilde, Taos, NM, http://www.LlamaAdventures.com.
9. See http://www.llamaadventures.com/whyllamas.html.
10. Charles Haddon Spurgeon, "Achsah's Asking, a Pattern of Prayer" No. 2312, http://bible.org/seriespage/achsah%E2%80%99s-asking-pattern-prayer-no-2312, delivered by Spurgeon at the Metropolitan Tabernacle, Newington, June 2, 1889.
11. See www.tomandpatcory.com.
12. See http://www.cummingsstudyguides.net/OurTown.html.
13. Tony Casteel and Robert Brewer, interviews with the author.
14. Corrie ten Boom, *Tramp for the Lord* (Jove Books, 1978), 55.
15. See http://www.newadvent.org/cathen/09604a.htm.
16. See http://www.neonatology.org/classics/old.terms.html and http://wordnetweb.princeton.edu/perl/webwn?s=manna.
17. See http://www.its.caltech.edu/~atomic/snowcrystals/alike/alike.htm.
18. Albert Schweitzer, *Memoirs of Youth and Childhood*, translated by Kurt Bergel and Alice R. Bergel (Syracuse University Press, 1997).
19. See http://atheism.about.com/od/religiousplaces/p/GardenGethsemane.htm.

Also available from Lynn Coulter

Mustard Seeds

Thoughts on the
Nature of God and Faith

A collection of fifteen essays about the natural graces and "God signs" that emerged during a three-year period of hardship and sustain her faith today. From personal events to universal cripplers, Coulter's fresh anecdotes unearth the little daily markers of God's love and care while staying rooted in Scripture.

Trade Paper // 192 pages // ISBN 978-0-8054-4678-4 // Retail Price $14.99